CREATING OUTDOOR THEATRE

CREATING OUTDOOR THEATRE

A Practical Guide

Nina Ayres

ROWOOD PRESS

First published in 2008 by
The Crowood Press Ltd
Ramsbury, Marlborough
Wiltshire SN8 2HR

www.crowood.com

British Library Cataloguing-in-Publication Data
A catalogue record for this book is available from the British Library.

ISBN 978 1 84797 045 9

Illustrations by Keith Field (pages 10, 11, 12, 15, 17, 20, 21) and Caroline Pratt (pages 19, 120, 121, 124, 125, 132, 133)

Frontispiece: World Famous' production at Winchester Hat Fair, 2005. (Photo: Jackie King)

Typeset by Jean Cussons Typesetting, Diss, Norfolk

Printed and bound in Malaysia by Times Offset (M) Sdn Bhd

CONTENTS

ACKNOWLEDGEMENTS

I would like to thank all my friends and family who supported me during the writing of this book. Thanks to all the theatre practitioners who took the time to have lengthy discussions with me about outdoor theatre and generously provided quotes and photographs to be used for publication. A special thanks to Tom for painstakingly going through the manuscript with a fine tooth comb and making it a much better product as a result!

FOREWORD

A Landscape of Change –
The Excitement of Creating
Outdoor Theatre

I
t is with great enthusiasm that I am writing this foreword. Finally, a book that is an essential guide for anyone who is excited about the prospect of expanding upon what they perceive as performance, by moving away from the structure and formality of fixed theatre spaces out into the open air. I myself have found the leap both liberating and challenging. It is such a different beast with such diverse opportunities and practicalities. I also believe that with Nina being a designer constantly working in this environment, she brings a holistic approach and totally up-to-date knowledge to explaining how to go about creating Outdoor Theatre.

My own keen interest began as a designer on several productions with undergraduate drama students, on a yearly project at the Minack Theatre in Cornwall. These were community-based productions often devised from

Keith Orton with colleagues exploring the dynamics of the countryside in South Wales.

local history, folklore or established children's stories. Working at such a unique theatre set on the cliffs of Porthcurno with its spectacular dramatic seascape throws into question the designer's role. In this type of environment, I believe that the production team needs truly to appreciate and analyse the resonance and the spatial qualities that are offered by the given environment before considering adding specific design elements. This has led me to question in greater detail the role of designer in proto-naturalistic landscapes. By proto-naturalistic, I mean landscapes that have been historically changed and manipulated by human intervention, working with the belief that there is no such thing as natural landscape.

Following on from this, for a three-year period, I have been found skulking around the borders of Wales on each bank-holiday weekend engaging in a series of performative experiments. Working with director Sally Mackey, I had the unique opportunity to work with a hugely creative set of performers/devisers whom she had previously brought together to perform a devised piece about the Arthurian legends as a tour around the Border Castles of Wales. Now we were able creatively to play and perform in a site that offered a wide range of different landscapes and social contexts. By using a field-study centre called Caer Llan, we were able to bring together our expertise to experiment with what we mean by performance that is driven directly by the qualities of the landscape itself. From this I have gained an understanding of design as visual dramaturgy, providing the visual stimulus for production rather than facilitating set and costume requirements.

I truly believe that when creating Outdoor Theatre it frees up anyone involved in its creation, everyone feels out of their comfort zone for multitudinous reasons. Unpredictable conditions promote ingenuity and we all find that inner child again. We are all given the permission to play!

Keith Orton

1 WHY OUTDOOR THEATRE?

Outdoor theatre is fast becoming one of the most talked about and popular forms of theatre in the modern day. It has seen a steady rise in popularity in the last few years as practitioners seek to reach a wider audience and experiment with the possibilities that an outdoor setting presents. Outdoor theatre is in no way a modern phenomenon. Indeed, theatre originated out of doors as a popular form of enlightenment and entertainment.

The earliest recorded evidence of theatre shows an art form that sought to engage people from all walks of life. It was often paid for by the wealthier members of society and offered freely to those less well off. Today, there is evidence of a similar trend emerging within our towns and cities as local councils stage

'Theatre has to connect, it has to engage and then perhaps it can educate. Indoor Theatre is limited – in audiences it reaches and the possibilities for wider connections with wider audiences, in wider contexts and for better developments of new forms and structures.'

(From a summary of discussion from Improbable Theatre's workshop in 2006, entitled *Disillusioned and Disgruntled*)

events, which include community involvement, or merely offer entertainment free of charge to every citizen. In the majority of cases, these productions are staged outside.

Staging a show outside immediately removes the barriers that often keep people away from theatre, as they believe it to be some kind of exclusive club for academically minded people. An outdoor theatre space is less intimidating, often with no formal seating arrangement, making it possible for people to come and go as they please. It often relies more heavily on performers' exaggerated gestures and on visuals rather than text to tell the narrative and can therefore communicate effectively to people on all levels.

THE ORIGINS OF THEATRE

There is evidence that every ancient society has a history of oral storytelling, which is passed from one generation to the next. The rituals and rites of passage often involved a performance or dance of some kind and included the wearing of costumes and masks.

The world's earliest recorded dramatic production is from ancient Egypt. Written on a stone tablet in about 2000 BC, it tells of a king's representative who acted out parts in a play about a god who suffered but triumphed in the end. The aim of this play, as is the case of most recorded examples of ancient drama, was to

9

Sticky, *an outdoor theatre piece by Improbable Theatre and the pyrotechnic company The World Famous, using local volunteers and lots of sticky tape.*

The Greek masks of comedy and tragedy (from original artwork of the period).

keep vivid in the minds of the faithful the sufferings and triumph of a god.

The central figure was the legendary king-divinity, Osiris, and plays in his memory were performed annually at Abydos, Busiris and Heliopolis. The acting at that time was apparently realistic as Greek historians tell us that many actor-warriors died of the wounds received in the 'mock' battles between the enemies of Osiris and the forces led by his son, Ap-uat. This play is regarded as the first 'passion play' in that it deals with life, death and resurrection. It is the precursor of many passion plays, including the Persian passion play of Hussein, the seventeenth-century Oberammergau in Germany concerning the life of Christ and the liturgical dramas that were performed in parts of Britain in medieval times.

ANCIENT HISTORY

Greece

The first evidence of what we understand as theatre comes from the ancient Greek civilization and dates back to the earliest plays of Aeschylus, around 500 BC.

Festivals

The ancient Greeks believed theatre to be a fundamental part of their life. Actors were paid by the state, and festivals were held up to three times a year, when new plays, written by, for example, Aeschylus, Sophocles – and later Aristophanes and Euripides – could be viewed. The most famous festival was held at the city of Dionysia, where prizes were awarded for excellence in acting or playwriting.

The cast and playwrights

Greek drama initially involved large casts who travelled from festival to festival on carts and played in the huge amphitheatres specifically built to house these productions. The content of the plays largely centred on the various

Ancient Greek actor in costume (from original artwork of the period).

Greek gods and their interaction with humans, although each playwright was known for his particular style. For example, Aeschylus' plays were powerful tragedies whereas Aristophanes was well known for the superb comic characters he created. Sophocles wrote humane plays focusing on the conflict between characters, and Euripides was predominantly political and social in his work.

Costumes

Greek actors wore elaborate, often padded theatrical costumes with high boots and headdresses to make them stand out in the huge, open-air arenas in which they performed. They often wore masks to enable them to play more than one role and to take on female characters. The wearing of masks meant that

11

they had to use their voice and physicality to portray the character, or, indeed, the animal they were playing.

Early Greek theatre involved a chorus of fifty people who would narrate the story through song and dance, but as playwrights introduced more actors into their dramas so this number decreased to twelve. The chorus wore lighter versions of the main actors' garments so that they would have more freedom of movement.

The performing area

The amphitheatres in which the festivals took place were elaborate, which shows just how important theatre was to the Greeks. They were well built and often equipped with trapdoors and cranes to enable the 'gods' to descend from above. From the examples still in existence, it's reasonable to suppose that the playing area for the actors consisted of a flat circle, an altar in the centre back for the chorus and musicians and a raked, semicircular seating area to house the audience. The stage often had, at the back, a building with entrance doors. This served various functions: as background to the actors, as an acoustic device that brought their voice forward, and as an area for quick changes and property store.

Ancient Rome

By the third century BC, a form of 'new

The Ancient Greek stage.

The remains of a Roman theatre at Autun, France.

comedy' had spread to Italy from Greece. The Roman playwright Plautus wrote comedies that were almost a direct translation of the Greek plays, but made relevant to Roman audiences. The taste for theatre was heading away from sophisticated content and towards more farcical drama.

As a result, the short rustic farces of *fabula atellana* in southern Italy became popular. This theatre introduced elaborately comic characters, including the clowns Maccus and Bucco, and is said to have been the inspiration behind the later Italian drama *commedia dell'arte*, which still has an enormous influence on today's acting styles. Although the Romans built beautiful and elaborate theatres, the plays degenerated into bawdy and obscene

'It seems difficult to understand the uncompromising attitude adopted towards the theatre by Christian writers of the early centuries. But the fact remains that all forms of the drama were banned indiscriminately and we can only infer that the plays and mimes popular under the Roman Empire were seen as grossly indecent. The surviving plays of Aristophanes would alone suffice to show how inconceivably lax public opinion was, while the *infamia* which marked the legal status of an actor at Rome is significant of the degradation involved by such a profession.'

(Herbert Thurston, *The Catholic Encyclopedia*, Volume XIV, published in 1912)

mimes. Consequently, the craft of acting and playwriting lost the respect in which it had been held, and the theatre was eventually banned altogether.

PAGANISM AND FOLK HISTORY

Seasonal celebrations

Some form of spirituality has always existed in cultures throughout the ages and still exists in some form in most cultures today. It is often centred on the solar manifestations of the summer and winter solstice and the spring and autumnal equinox. These seasonal turning points are marked with celebrations based around the various ideas of year's end and year's beginning, death and rebirth, and sowing and reaping. This belief system assumes that supernatural forces are in control and should be commemorated in order to secure the health and prosperity of a community or an individual.

Folklore or ritual

Ancient folklore used theatrical techniques and role-play to appease the spirit world. Re-enactment of the roles of evil or destructive forces called for the creation of grotesque masks and demonic costumes – and the use of noisy instruments to drive them away.

Harvest figures were often made to call upon the spirits for a good crop yield, and special foods in symbolic shapes were prepared and consumed. According to the culture, many other accessories were created: decorated trees and poles, lanterns, banners, processional vehicles, sculptured figures or dolls and household and shrine adornments. These all bore the motifs of life symbolism.

It can be argued that this type of ritual or folklore cannot be seen as a form of theatre because people believed the ceremonies were crucial to their survival, not a means of

enlightenment or enjoyment. However, it does form the roots for many types of outdoor theatre which have existed since and displays the themes of community spirit and attachment to the earth. The green man festival, for instance has celebrated the coming of summer throughout the ages through various plays and dances performed outside. Pagan rituals which celebrate the earth and our place on it through the use of masks and 'offerings' have developed through the centuries and become incorporated into mummers' plays and plays which tell of folklore history. The church itself also recognized that there was a primitive desire among the common people to perform festive rituals, particularly at the spring planting time and the harvest season. It is no coincidence that the 'miracle' and 'mystery' play cycles began to be performed at precisely these seasonal turning points.

MEDIEVAL DRAMA

The major resurgence in theatre began in the Middle Ages with small rituals being performed by the clergy inside the church in celebration of the resurrection. At a time when there were no other means of mass communication and church services were conducted in Latin, dramatising the Bible was a way of familiarising people with its contents and getting its message across. In time, these rituals gave way to much bigger, full-scale pageants that were performed outdoors – and by the faithful rather than the clergy. This shift to the outdoors came about partly because scenarios were increasingly elaborate and required more space, although there is some evidence to suggest that dialogue had become more vulgar and was no longer considered appropriate for the church interior.

Liturgical dramas were also enacted in Europe's Christian nations, and were known as *sacre rappresentazioni* in Italy, *autos sacra-*

A Mediaeval pageant wagon.

mentales in Spain, *Geistspiele* in Germany and *mystères* in France.

Miracle plays

Miracle plays developed from Biblical re-enactments by the clergy in churches after the Pope forbade, in 1210, clerical participation in such plays. Faithful members of the church thus took over the presentation of the plays, at first inside the church, but increasingly the concept was taken on by groups who began performing the plays on sites in rural communities. The subject matter of the plays was the miracles performed by saints and scenes from the Bible.

An amphitheatre called Plen-an-Gwary in St Just, Cornwall, has evidence to show that

> 'The mystery plays are essentially popular art, designed for large mass audiences in open spaces.'
>
> (Sir Peter Hall, theatre director)

Cornish miracle plays took place there until about 1600.

Mystery plays

Records suggest that the English mystery plays, or cycles, evolved from the late fourteenth century onwards. The cycles, which were made up of a number of individual pageants, were usually performed in celebration of the early summer feast of Corpus Christi. At first, the mystery plays were performed by priests and took place inside churches and cathedrals, but once they were taken outside, tradesmen's guilds (or Mysteries) began to sponsor particular plays and the players themselves became the guild members.

Records from York and Chester indicate that the plays were performed on pageant wagons, which were wheeled through the city streets and brought to a halt at certain points or 'stations' around the town. There is also evidence to suggest that these plays were performed on the move, in a semicircle, as a line of stages or in the round as was often the case in Cornwall.

15

'The mystery plays may be regarded as the most democratic thing in English literature. Whatever may have been their original conception, they became in fact in the middle ages, of the people, by the people, for the people.'

(Godfrey W. Mathews,
The Chester Mystery Plays)

For several centuries immense amounts of money, time and effort were expended on producing these cycles of Biblical plays. At Chester, the cycle took three days to perform and at York, the cycle, which used up to forty-eight wagons, could only be mounted on Corpus Christi day by using all the hours of daylight at the summer equinox.

Mounting the cycles demanded a vast communal and civic endeavour, and was fuelled by inter-guild competitiveness. Carts or 'pageants' were often two storeys high and could include complicated trapdoors and, like their Greek predecessors, cranes to lower 'God' from above. Livestock was often used in the telling of the stories, and the use of masks was prevalent. The Devil was often grotesquely comical, while the angels and God wore beautiful, gilded masks. The guilds often presented appropriate stories; so for example the shipwrights were responsible for the Building of the Ark, while the butchers played the Death of Christ and the fishmongers the story of Jonah and the Whale. The plays taught a simple message and were written to appeal to all sections of the community. They were extremely sophisticated and often visually lavish.

These popular spectacles later spawned smaller companies of six to nine men who travelled around performing scaled-down versions of the plays at religious sites and on city streets. These became known as 'Morality plays'. Gradually, these companies became intertwined with other travelling players performing various forms of popular entertainment.

THE RENAISSANCE

In Italy, in the fourteenth century, there was a revival of the works of the ancient Greeks and Romans, and theatre reverted to classical drama. But impromptu outdoor stages were simply not suitable to house such dramas. In an attempt to present these plays in their original manner, theatres were built that were considered to be versions of ancient Greek and Roman architecture. Unlike the majority of Roman theatres, however, these structures were often rectangular and covered by a pitched roof.

Advancements in staging were soon made, and the proscenium arch and painted flat scenery emerged. Huge efforts were made to replicate the outdoors by building the 'sky' over the stage and 'flying' the clouds in. Since many of these plays were read in Latin, this was not popular theatre but was aimed at an educated audience.

Commedia dell'arte

While spectacular performances were being performed for the aristocracy, the general public had its own companies of players, who erected trestle platforms in the open streets. Beginning during the Renaissance and lasting into the eighteenth century, travelling troupes performed the *commedia dell' arte* and worked on the premise of having stock characters and situations around which the performers improvised. The actors wore distinctive clothing and small, half masks, and each actor played the same roles the whole of his life.

The actors employed acrobatic skills and performed in a fast and furious fashion, using satire to ridicule characters whom the audi-

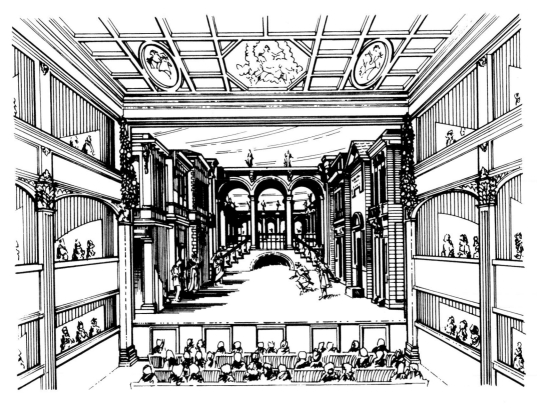

The Italian Renaissance stage.

ence would recognize. *Commedia dell'arte* troupes travelled all over Europe, sometimes using their portable stages in villages and towns, but eventually they were invited to perform in the halls and palaces of Europe.

TEMPORARY OUTDOOR THEATRE

As a result of a ban brought about by the Reformation, the acting of religious plays came to an end in England in the fifteenth century. Consequently, bands of professional players began to form and started touring the festivals and fairs. These were sometimes referred to as interlude players. They per-

formed chronicle plays, which largely worked to the same formula as the mystery plays, but enacted stories from English history rather than the Bible.

Temporary platforms were set up as stages in the yards of inns and taverns or any place where an audience could congregate. Inn yards were especially popular as refreshment was readily available, and inns often had balconies that could be used to separate the more affluent members of society from the often-rowdy mob at ground level.

During the fifteenth and sixteenth centuries, 'high days' and holidays came into existence to mark the crossroads in farming activity. An assortment of farces, jigs and

17

Photograph of the yard at The George Inn in Southwark, London, showing the balconies where the wealthier clientele would sit to watch the play in the courtyard.

comical musical performances, known as drolls, were played on temporary booth stages in towns and villages across Europe. The practice of singing religious verse to popular ballad tunes also emerged in the mid-sixteenth century, but it was not popular with all members of the general public.

Mumming or mummers' plays

From the fourteenth century onwards, mumming or mummers' plays were popular dramatic entertainment in which a popular hero of the time was killed in a fight and then brought back to life by a doctor. It is thought

'For so impudent and irreligious are many in these Times growne, that I have heard in foolish and ridiculous Ballads (whose makers and publishers deserve a whipping) the name of our blessed Saviour, invocated and sung to those roguish tunes, which have formerly served for profane jiggs; An impiety odious to a good Christian; and yet use hath made it so familiar that we can now heare it, and scarce take notice that there is ought evill therein.'

(George Wither, sixteenth century)

that the plays were linked to the primitive ceremonies that were held to mark important
stages in the agricultural year. Masks were
often used in mummers' plays, which became
known as guizes. In order to remain anony-
mous, the actors' faces were – and still often
are – hidden by ribbons or plaited straw, or
darkened with dirt. The actors were then free
to satirize the inequalities of wealth and mock
the aristocracy. If any offence arose from the
mumming, the identity of the mummer was
therefore hidden, so saving him from blame.

It is thought that the word mumming may
have originated from 'mumble', either because

*Modern-day mummers at the Green Man
Festival in Hastings. (Photo: Simon Costin)*

One of the commedia dell'arte *characters,
Arlecchino (c. 1671), later known as
Harlequin, from an engraving by
A. Manceau.*

the actor could not be clearly heard from
behind the mask or because the action was
performed without words, so that the actors
were essentially 'keeping mum'.

Travelling players

Wandering players continued to travel and
perform throughout the sixteenth century.
Just as Germany and France received English
troupes at their annual fairs so companies
returned to England with new ideas. The
troupes normally consisted of four men and a
boy, who played all the female roles since
women were not allowed to perform.

As theatrical ideas started to move across
the channel, Covent Garden saw the first
puppet booth show from Italy, with characters
taken from *commedia dell' arte*, including

19

Pulcinella, who developed into Punch. This performance was later adapted to an English audience and came to be known as Punch and Judy.

THE MOVE TOWARDS PERMANENT STRUCTURES

Towards the end of the sixteenth century, the authorities became increasingly strict in their dealings with the travelling players. This cre-ated a need for permanent structures within their control. In 1576, James Burbage built the first permanent theatre in England. An actor and under the protection of the Lord Chamberlain, Burbage built the open-roofed theatre, 'the theatre in the open fields' outside the London city limits.

This building was the first of many similar theatres, the most famous being the Globe (also by Burbage) and the Swan. Not much is known about the original wooden structures,

A copy of Johannes de Witt's sketch of the Swan theatre of c.1596, showing the typical Elizabethan theatre interior.

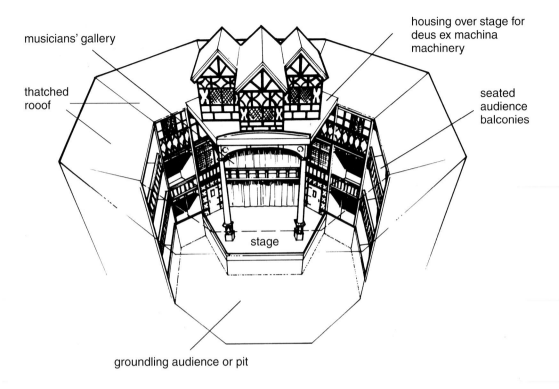

musicians' gallery

housing over stage for
deus ex machina
machinery

thatched
rooof

seated
audience
balconies

stage

groundling audience or pit

The Elizabethan playhouse.

but it is thought they were unroofed with raised platforms around the edge. A central space opened out for the standing audience and, around, there were tiered galleries for seated patrons. This design replicated the galleries that had often been a feature of the inn yards.

The actors were protected from the weather by a canopy over the stage. There was also a balcony, as in Greek and Roman theatres, behind the playing area and probably for use by musicians or in balcony scenes. The entrance fee of one penny for 'groundlings' made these theatres accessible to a much larger section of the general public, and the content of the plays was often considered coarse by the middle classes.

Christopher Marlowe, Ben Jonson and William Shakespeare all wrote for open-air public theatres like the Globe and the Swan, but by the turn of the seventeenth century, many plays were written for private or indoor theatres. England's first indoor theatre was established at Blackfriars in 1796, and was

'Romantically I like to think theatre started out of doors then sort of got caught. After a period of confinement it became tamed then its keepers sold tickets to visitors.'

(Jonathan Petherbridge,
London Bubble Theatre Company)

21

intended as a winter alternative to the Globe for the Lord Chamberlain's men (of whom William Shakespeare was one). The seats were comparatively expensive and therefore attracted a smaller and more educated audience.

Theatre Moves Inside

From the mid-nineteenth century, London's West End began to develop comfortable seating, better facilities and a more refined repertory, which attracted the middle classes back to the theatre. By 1900, most theatres were lit by electricity and the auditorium darkened during the performance. The stage was invariably framed by the proscenium arch and separated from the auditorium by an orchestra pit.

Indoor theatre expanded rapidly and outdoor theatre was seen as outmoded and unfashionable. The idea of choosing to play outdoors seemed ludicrous when there was an ever-increasing number of comparatively luxurious indoor venues in which to perform.

The theatre became an elite pastime both in Britain and in Europe and it wasn't until the beginning of the twentieth century that many theatre practitioners sought ways to break the mould.

New designers emerged who were dissatisfied with the Victorian theatre aesthetic of a naturalistic, painted backcloth, and they began to look at ways to break away from the norm. In the 1920s, Gordon Craig and Adolph Appia were at the forefront of these changes and experimented with new stage configurations away from the proscenium arch. Although they never took theatre back outside, a desire for a new type of theatre was developing, with a growing interest in using outdoor space once again. The mystery plays were being rediscovered and remounted, and Shakespeare's plays were also seeing a revival.

'Transformance is a performative process which involves an entire milieu or community. Theatre becomes the active force that can revitalize a community, uncovering the hidden bonds as well as the socializing cultural processes which characterize it. The designation professional/non-professional is erased. The multiplicity of subcultures becomes visible as they present themselves to each other.'

(Eugenio Barba, director, Odin Theatre)

The 1960s Onwards

It was not until the 1960s that a considerable interest in outdoor theatre re-emerged. It's not a coincidence that so many of the outdoor theatre companies that have become the benchmark of what is performed today started in the 1960s. Disillusioned by the elitism of the theatre (and too political to be allowed into conservative, indoor theatres), new companies emerged, wanting to take their theatre out onto the streets.

One theatre company at the forefront of this change in attitude was Odin Theatre from Denmark. Taking its influence from shamanic rituals and ceremonies, it chose to perform in unusual places, such as on the street or in the open air, and, specifically, in socially discriminated areas. The company wanted the theatre to be placed in a specific context in order to give it political value, and this type of theatre came to be known as 'site specific'.

Likewise, companies such as People Show and Welfare State International began to perform in 'non-venues', specifically because they weren't welcome in traditional venues. They felt that using the architectural landscape of towns and cities as a natural stage could help to bridge the gap between formal theatre and everyday life. They shared a

'Welfare State International is brilliant at making an audience of strangers into a community.'

(Lyn Gardner, *The Guardian*)

common goal of wanting to celebrate the dramatic changes in mood and motion of these spaces and to reclaim them as communal, public arenas for the whole community to enjoy.

Ever since the 1960s, theatre companies with a drive to bring theatre back to the people and to use unconventional and outdoor spaces have been on the increase. The last fifty years has seen a dramatic shift in attitudes from companies performing outside as a matter of practicality to companies choosing to perform outside as a matter of preference.

The emergence of community theatre and community plays in the 1970s began to involve whole communities in the staging of plays. Gradually, theatre touched the lives of whole areas of the population that might never otherwise have come into contact with it. Outdoor festivals also sprang up, encompassing not only staged music performances but also whole dramatic works and celebra-

'Working outside gives us a great deal of independence. We don't have to do what the industry dictates. We don't have to split income. We can work in a field if we want and split income with the birds. It's just us (if we want it that way), and our audience. Because we work with communities many people come to our shows because it's a village event and not because they are theatre-goers. We are often their only experience of professional theatre. This may or may not be true if we were in the village hall. I think probably not. Being outdoors with your community may be an ancient rite. The village green is a holy place. I think we are closer outdoors, far more than we ever could be indoors to people who may be intimidated by conventional theatre spaces. But the usual theatre-goers are there too, so we are bringing people together.'

(Pete Talbot,
The Rude Mechanical Theatre Company)

tions connected with nature and the seasons. This trend, along with the development of new ideas on how to stage theatre, has created a whole host of styles, techniques and staging configurations blended into outdoor as well as indoor shows.

2 TYPES OF OUTDOOR THEATRE

There are many types of outdoor theatre, catering for almost every taste, and performances vary enormously. Each year the boundaries are pushed further, creating theatre that is increasingly unconventional in setting and style. As explored in the previous chapter, amphitheatres and purpose-built performance spaces have existed for centuries, but these now only account for a fraction of the venues that are used today.

Since the late 1960s, the interest in staging performances out of doors has increased rapidly. It has recently been described as 'one of the fastest-growing sectors in British arts'. The benefits of this kind of performance and its wide-reaching appeal have become all too evident, and the art form has really begun to take on a life of its own. The types of shows in these diverse 'venues' are now as varied as the sites themselves. There are also increasingly different practitioners becoming involved in wanting to stage an outdoor production – and for a myriad of reasons.

The type and scale of productions that are staged out of doors vary enormously – from a small, one-handed show to a huge spectacle involving a cast of hundreds. Of course, both can be seen as outdoor theatre so long as there is a story, or narrative, being expressed either visually or orally. If there is no story in the production, it falls under the heading of 'outdoor performance'. For the purposes of this book, I will look purely at 'outdoor theatre'.

WHO PRODUCES THE WORK?

Some established outdoor theatre venues produce their own shows every season, whereas others invite only outdoor theatre companies to tour to their venue. Theatre companies often produce complete shows, which can be self-contained and performed practically anywhere. These can range from something fairly small-scale, such as from the back of a truck, including everything from the set to the lighting rig, to something huge that takes days or even weeks at the site to set up and rehearse.

Some companies produce shows for a particular site or venue and tailor the show accordingly. Theatre companies sometimes travel to outdoor theatre festivals, which are often hosted by a local council or are part of a bigger event. Some companies however, have an established reputation and tour alone, gaining permission to use specific sites suitable for their particular show. Companies that are fortunate are funded by the lottery, the Arts Council or private funding bodies, whereas others have to rely merely on ticket sales.

There are an increasing number of theatre groups that tackle social issues, and some produce shows with specific agendas. Other companies will work with people from the community to produce a show together. These shows can be sponsored or commissioned by public or private companies, and sometimes a steering committee is set up within the community to raise funds.

How the Work is Devised

The initial impetus for putting on an outdoor show is almost identical to that of a conventional theatre company. The way it is produced usually falls into one of the following categories:

A piece of established text is taken and worked upon to suit the needs of the company, audience and environment. This can be anything from an ancient script to a modern play or adaptation.

A piece is written for or by the company beforehand, either to exploit its particular talents or to explore a particular theme or location.

A piece is devised by the company, and the show is produced from that process. This can either be in text form, written by a writer involved in the process, or manipulated by the director to produce a suitable performance. Sometimes the devising process has an idea, theme or location as the starting point.

Any one of the techniques listed above, or indeed a blend of them, can be used to find the narrative, and each technique can produce a

'Sometimes we bring the seeds of a narrative to a site, sometimes we'll look for the seeds in the landscape and the people we meet.'

(Bill Mitchel, artistic director of WildWorks about its approach to devising)

successful outcome. However, one technique may lend itself better to a particular theme, a particular group of performers or even a particular audience.

Outdoor Settings

We now see plays taking place in every conceivable nook and cranny of our surroundings: lakes, rivers, farms, streets, gardens, parks, woodlands, castles, caverns – and even beaches – now play host to a variety of theatrical styles.

'The sloping beach is a natural amphitheatre sloping down to a flat beach that, with the sea at low tide, becomes a huge stage of shallow rolling waves and reflective wet sand.'

(Small Wonder Theatre Company)

With such huge scope to perform practically anywhere outside, a whole range of exciting possibilities opens up to theatre practitioners. We can match our theatrical environment almost identically with that of the play's setting so that everything – the set, lighting and sound – will work in perfect harmony with the play itself. The setting of the sun, the rustling of the wind, the crashing of the waves or even the blue sky above cannot be recreated with such precision in a traditional indoor venue. Consequently, outdoor venues have taken on a significant part of the designer's job, so long as the designer is true to the environment and fully exploits its potential.

Working with the Environment

Non purpose-built spaces can easily be transformed into an arena with little more than the focusing of attention by an audience. This is

'The audience mainly don't know each other, except within their discrete groups. They compete for temporary ownership of a piece of ground and sit in circles or semi-circles. Definitely not rows. They take out whole meals, tables, cutlery, candelabra even, and hold court. Then the players come in to entertain them. Preferably Shakespeare, Mozart or some other incontestable classic. They are taking part in a quaint English ritual inspired by ideas of Edwardian times with the butler taking the hamper out of the boot of a classic car. For a while they own that place, that castle, that play, that opera. It is a culture game.'

(Pete Talbot, artistic director, The Rude Mechanical Theatre Company)

not necessarily a reason to choose to do a show outside. Of course, budget implications apply but all too often with outdoor theatre it is far too easy for companies to become complacent and to let the setting do all the hard work for them. Theatre companies should be wary of merely offering a backdrop to a social gathering, simply because the audience can take in the air, drink some champagne and enjoy a picnic. If spectators are more engaged with their plate than the production, then the company has comprehensively failed to produce a successful piece of outdoor theatre.

The setting should present possibilities to the group, but crucially, it needs to go beyond what can be achieved indoors. Rather than being a safer option, outdoor theatre requires the group to work harder in almost all other

The Spirit of Shivarre, 1990. *A Colway Theatre Trust community play for the Eramosa township in Ontario, Canada. (Photo: Jon Oram)*

aspects to make the show a success and to question why an outdoor space is being used. An outdoor theatre location does not have to be beautiful or majestic, as is often assumed. The space can be challenging, uncomfortable or even edgy. It can be an industrial site or a graveyard, for example, so long as it is safe for an audience and is chosen for its innate dynamics, which suit the requirements of the piece.

PERMANENT OUTDOOR VENUES

Permanent outdoor venues include established outdoor theatre venues such as The Globe Theatre on London's Southbank, the Regent's Park Open Air Theatre and the Minack Theatre in Cornwall. These, like many permanent outdoor venues, are only open for the summer season between May and September. Some permanent outdoor venues, like some conventional theatres, often specialize in a particular genre.

The Globe Theatre

The Globe Theatre, a replica of Shakespeare's original playhouse dating from 1599, usually performs six plays per season, shown in rotation. This is a fairly unusual timetable, but works well in maximizing ticket sales to tourists and allows rest time for the actors. Of these six plays, four are usually Shakespearian and two are more contemporary. The Globe produces the shows in-house and works with professional actors and technicians.

Despite its incredible historical setting, the Globe Theatre often produces challenging adaptations of Shakespeare's work, pushing his plays into relevant modern-day situations and exploiting the dynamic relationship between the audience and actors. With the majority of audience members standing in the centre pit as 'groundlings', they are close enough to rest their chins on the edge of the stage, and a great atmosphere is created as the 'them' and 'us' barrier becomes less apparent.

Regent's Park Open Air Theatre

Regent's Park Theatre, established in 1932, works in a similar way. It normally has four shows per season, produced by its professional in-house company. Two of these plays are Shakespearian, one is a musical and one a children's play. Both the Globe and Regent's Park are fully equipped with lighting, sound rigs and permanent seating, identical to many indoor theatre venues.

The Minack Theatre

The Minack Theatre in Cornwall was built into the edge of a cliff in 1932. It has incredible views across Porthcurno Bay and runs its theatre programme in a very different way from the Globe Theatre and Regent's Park Theatre. Although it is fully equipped, albeit on a less spectacular scale, it books only outside and touring theatre companies. It has a policy to book new and sometimes inexperienced companies, mainly from the Cornwall area. This policy creates exciting opportunities for new and diverse companies, whilst keeping ticket prices down.

The stunning location and arrangement of the seating, in an amphitheatre above the stage, creates a wonderful natural backdrop to the shows. Unlike the other permanent theatres mentioned above, this theatre poses extreme weather considerations. For example, the wind can whip across the bay and the 'open' nature of the stage renders the use of backdrops and scenic elements cause for careful consideration.

TOURING PRODUCTIONS

A touring show is one that has been created by a company and is then taken to and performed

27

Regent's Park Open Air Theatre, production of A Midsummer Night's Dream, *2006.*

BELOW: *The Rude Mechanical Theatre Company's performance of* Goldrush, *2006, Tunbridge Wells.*

in various venues around an area, country or countries. Whether a show tours locally or internationally will depend on the size and often the success of the theatre piece or company. Some theatre shows will tour to a number of different outdoor locations. The selection of these locations can either be a random affair or fit within the parameters of the company's ideology or the specifics of the show.

A good example is The Rude Mechanical Theatre Company, based in Sussex. It favours taking its *commedia dell' arte* style shows to small towns and villages in the south of England. The company's principal mission is 'to bring professional touring theatre to small rural communities' as a way of engaging people in performance who might normally never venture into a theatre. The Company also prefers using communal land, such as village greens and recreation grounds, to regain the historical use of these sites.

INDOOR AND OUTDOOR VENUES

Theatre groups sometimes include both indoor and outdoor venues on their tours and are aware of the different atmosphere that each creates. Each venue is different in its innate qualities and will impart its personality onto a piece. Therefore the show will be viewed differently by the audience from venue to venue. By its very nature, a show will look extremely different out of doors. Actors will have to adapt their performance style, and an outdoor audience behaves very differently from one in a formal, indoor setting.

Actors and technicians of theatre companies that tour both indoor and outdoor venues have to be skilled at equipping themselves for the huge differences that exist between the two. Sets made for indoor venues can be dwarfed by the great outdoors and, often, are

not strong enough to cope with challenging weather. Intricate dialogue and subtleties in narrative can be lost outside, as can knowing glances thrown between actors. The audience for a piece of outdoor theatre will respond to the informal setting by becoming more involved with the action and less insecure about the formal boundaries.

Some experienced theatre companies, such as Kneehigh, based in Cornwall, make this transition brilliantly from indoor to outdoor venue, but it isn't a simple task. The Company's vast experience in storytelling and performance makes it appear easy. It is very visual in its approach to theatre, and this goes some way to making it possible to include both indoor and outdoor venues in its tour schedule – as with the tour of *Cymbeline* in association with the Royal Shakespeare Company in 2006.

SITE GENERIC

Some companies successfully use a generic site for all performances. Each show will inevitably have some sort of criteria that need to be fulfilled at each venue, the most important being the size of the space. However, some shows require more specific attributes such as woodland, or a vast field with a wooden hut in the distance. The terms 'site generic' and 'site sensitive' refer to places that have a commonality. This way, the spectators are more likely to have a similar experience in each venue, and, in order to match its original themes or driving force, the company controls this experience.

'Site sensitive is a good term – we tour but utilize the gifts of each given location. Promenade usually.'

(Jonathan Petherbridge, London Bubble Theatre Company)

TOURING

Touring a show can be a fascinating way of seeing how it is perceived in different venues and then using this information to gain experience or to make more considered judgements for future tours. It can be an interesting experiment, but it is always better to make sound decisions from the start to avoid using your audience as critical guinea pigs. As well as the venues bringing their own personality to the performance, it has to be noted that an outdoor performance can alter dramatically from one day to the next – even if everything, from the location to the actors, stays the same.

An outdoor audience often becomes involved in the action. The very nature of being outside, as opposed to the often-rigid structure of an indoor theatre, loosens an audience's inhibitions and viewers are much more inclined to be vocal. Outdoor theatre audiences are more likely to cheer the 'goodies' and 'boo-hiss' the 'baddies', even in a relatively formal outdoor theatre venue such as the Globe Theatre.

NON-TOURING AND SITE SPECIFIC

If a show is not touring, then the possibility of producing a site-specific piece opens up. In some way this type of performance lets the environment inform the action or content. A site-specific piece of theatre pays special consideration to the site in which the theatre space is located. It has to take into account

Pushing the boundaries between everyday life and theatre in Metamorphosis by London Bubble Theatre Company in Sydenham Wells Park, London, 2006.

Site-specific piece of theatre called **Souterrain** *by WildWorks, as part of the Brighton Festival in Stamner village, 2006. The set is perfectly in tune with the 'natural' backdrop.*

everything about the place: its history, fauna and flora, geology and geography, aesthetics and dimensions.

A site-specific show aims to exploit the dynamic relationship with the environment in which it is played. In Richard Schechner's revolutionary paper, *Six Axioms of Environmental Theatre*, published in 1968, he outlines two different ways of using a space:

> In the first case one creates an environment by transforming a space; in the second case, one negotiates with an environment, engaging in a scenic dialogue with the space.'

In his first point, the action is 'indifferent' to the space, or vice versa. But in his second point, the action and the place can be reciprocal or in conflict with each other so that the activity disturbs the notion of the space.

Indifference to the space

Outdoor touring companies will sometimes use their surroundings merely as an empty stage. Almost in direct contrast to a site-specific piece, the environment is created in the same way that a set is built for the stage. This type of show almost completely ignores what is around or only uses the site for the

31

elements it needs and changes the ones it doesn't. It would be quite rare, if not impossible, for a company to change the site completely. The innate qualities of an environment are found not only in the land, the buildings and the trees, but also in the sounds, the air, the sky and the history surrounding it.

I have never seen a theatre company take on the challenge of changing most of the elements, so a huge amount of the site's personality is inevitable with each and every outdoor performance. Theatre companies can find it extremely difficult to find a site that matches their specific requirements exactly, and it

therefore makes perfect sense that the site will be altered in some way to help the audience's understanding of the piece. However, companies should always seek permission before the sight is changed in any way, especially if it permanently changes the look or function of the site.

Reciprocity of the space

If the environment can be used naturally to 'house' the show, without much, if anything, needing to be done in terms of set, the action and the place are said to be reciprocal. Theatre companies can even use real time within the

Incisor Productions' performance of Noel Coward's **Blithe Spirit**, *St Ann's Well Gardens, Hove, shows the indifference of the set design to the natural environment.*

show and take advantage of the changing light or the setting sun to work with their performance.

It is possible to give a piece of land a false significance so that the audience cannot distinguish between fact and fantasy/folklore. Theatre companies can dramatically change the relationship between reality and the 'theatre' in an outdoor setting, which is almost impossible in an indoor theatre. By using the site reciprocally, an audience can be thoroughly absorbed in the environment and story in immensely powerful ways.

Conflict in the space

Conversely, the environment can be used to contrast the action of the performance and thereby create a conflict between the two. Whether the company examines the site and works with its innate qualities or deliberately works against them is a decision that will have a profound effect on the piece of work.

> 'Site specific is totally inspired by the site, the show comes from the site, the site speaks what it speaks to you and you make a piece of work in response to that site.'
>
> (Paul Pinson, Boilerhouse)

Contrasting the place and action challenges both the audience's perception of the space and its function. For example, putting a boat full of sailors into a landscape that's miles from the sea becomes out of context and interesting in its own right. The audience will immediately be actively involved in thinking and questioning the reasons for it being there. The dislocation and unfamiliarity of contradicting a site allows the audience to make no assumptions and invites them to experience things innocently.

The colours that a designer introduces to the space in terms of set, costume and lighting can either jar with the site for a specific reason or blend with it and bring the elements of the performance into context with the space and unify the piece as a whole.

Mixing reciprocity and conflict

Some theatre companies will be reciprocal with a site in some aspects, or at some points during the show, while conflicting with it at others. This can sometimes make the contrast more shocking when it does happen, and can also be used to great comic effect. Imagine a space has a natural axis for actors to pass through, and this is adhered to throughout the show. Then suddenly an actor breaks through the space. The dramatic effect will be more apparent and signify something that sets him apart from all the other actors, or disassociates him with the function of the space. For example, if a path is set to represent the land and the grass represents the sea, the illusion can be broken by an actor suddenly strolling across the grass as if walking on water.

PROMENADE PERFORMANCE

A type of performance that often works well to

> 'The actor is as fearful of encouraging the participation of the audience as the audience is of participating. So there has been little incentive to research this relationship. Yet once you remove fixed seating and the automatic separation of space they create, entirely new relationships are possible, body contact can occur between performers and audience; voice levels and acting intensities can be varied widely; the sense of a shared experience can be engendered.'
>
> (Jon Oram, artistic director, Claque Theatre Company)

An ex-graduate company from the Central School of Speech and Drama preparing a set that is in conflict with the surrounding area. Part of the Caer Llan research project, Caer Llan, Wales. (Photo: Keith Orton)

show the different characteristics of the scenes is 'promenade'. Promenade performances either take the audience on the journey with them to the different 'lands' of the show, or simply work around or through the audience. It is the opposite of a conventional theatre set-up, as the audience has physically to 'move' to see the next setting, rather than the set changing to transform the scene. Audiences remain quite active throughout promenade performances and this can affect their attitude. They will invariably be more animated than a normal, static audience and may be more susceptible to participation.

Theatre companies often include characters or set pieces to help guide the audience and keep it engaged with the action while they travel between scenes. A great example of this was explored recently by a WildWorks production entitled *Souterrain*, which described the audience's journey as 'following the action through a living stage set'. The audience followed the actor's search for his love and were guided through a churchyard, farm buildings and hidden corners of a village.

At one stage, audience members were invited to write their own memories and add them to a collection of memories. They were then asked to walk through a series of installations created by the occupants of the village. These installations were monuments to the villagers' loved ones, displayed on their front lawns, which echoed the plight of the performer and helped to mark the journey. This personal involvement by the audience gave the whole piece a rather more intimate feel. Promenade performances have the unique ability physically to 'travel' with the audience and, because of the physical commitment required, become very real.

'I don't think this form (outdoor promenade theatre) is right for all theatre, and London Bubble regularly makes work for conventional theatre spaces. But for some pieces the action of placing a story in an environment that is neutral – that belongs more to the children who play there in the daytime than it does to the theatre company – is healthy. It ventilates and makes accessible an art form that has become separated from the vast majority of society. There are opportunities and benefits for performers, technicians, marketers and, undoubtedly, audiences.'

(Jonathan Petherbridge, artistic director, London Bubble Theatre Company)

TYPE AND SCALE OF PRODUCTION

The themes of theatre performances or public events are wide-ranging, concerning, for example, education, health, citizenship, racial harmony, community identity, literacy or local history. These themes have all been explored in outdoor venues, either from devised or scripted texts. There is a niche for the whole range of possible production styles with performances by actors and non-actors alike, and productions can be anything from huge extravaganzas using fireworks to intimate shows with tiny casts.

Invisible theatre

Brazilian director, Augusto Boal, coined the term 'invisible theatre' to describe the method whereby actors act like members of society to create drama. Invisible theatre rarely follows a narrative or performs a 'show' as we would understand it with a beginning, middle and an end. Instead, groups – of which the Natural Theatre Company is an example – improvise

around a theme and take on characters to interact with members of the public. This often has hilarious consequences, but is not outdoor theatre in the way that I have described it.

Spectacle

Another form of outside performance is called 'spectacle'. This covers large-scale events that often involve fireworks, pyrotechnics and/or water. Dazzling displays are designed, often involving circus skills or large-scale puppets, but there is no narrative. The spectacle is watched by spectators, which implies a passive role as no response is required from the audience. Outdoor theatre has a narrative and therefore requires an active audience.

The Bell *by Periplum and The World Famous pyrotechnics company, Alexandra Park, Hastings, 2007. (Photo: Deborah Pearson)*

Beyond spectacle

Some theatre companies take spectacle a step further to create stunning, large-scale outdoor theatre shows involving tangible stories. Improbable Theatre Company recently toured a show called *Sticky*, whereby a huge set was created in front of the audience using hundreds of metres of sticky tape. It was then destroyed by the sparks and flames of fireworks and pyrotechnics. From this destruction emerged hundreds of balloons along with a human figure in the guise of an insect, who was raised by a crane high above the heads of the audience. Although the show had large-scale visuals, a metaphor was created, giving it a theatrical content that went beyond spectacle.

'The piece had a slow pace which allowed an image to stay in the audience's mind. The outdoor audience seemed to be prepared to watch and wait much more than an indoor audience would. We created a fairly loose story to enable the audience to read any number of meanings into the piece.'

(Lee Simpson, Improbable Theatre Company)

Community theatre

An interesting aspect of *Sticky* is the fact that the 'performers' and some of the technical crew who built the tower of sticky tape were members of the local community. They had

The Princess, the Palace and the Ice Cold Bath, *a community play performed in Claremont, Surrey, involving a cast of more than 150 local people. (Photo: Keith Orton)*

A scene from the York Mystery Plays, 2002.

volunteered to work with the company while it was in town, and consequently, they learned their puppetry, performance and technical skills from the company professionals. This type of skill-sharing is called community theatre. Community theatre differs from amateur theatre in that it is produced, written, directed, designed and facilitated in large part by professional theatre practitioners, who pass on their necessary skills to produce the show.

Community theatre isn't necessarily always out of doors, but it lends itself well to this medium. It can accommodate a very large cast if the community theatre company has an inclusive policy, i.e. that no person who wants to be in the show is turned away. Its scripts are often about the history of the community, and therefore, by staging the show on the soil they communally occupy, it is making a poignant statement.

The community may be asked to research the local history, come up with ideas through improvisation, help to make the set, costumes and props, assist technically and ultimately perform in the show. This will all be done under the supervision of a core professional team. Community theatre is often funded in part by the local council, the lottery or other arts bodies (although the community itself may need to raise further funds).

Amateur societies

An amateur dramatic society usually runs its own company without a professional team, much like the mystery plays of the past did. In keeping with that same tradition, members of an amateur society often have skills or trades that are utilized as and when the show requires. Amateur societies mostly perform established scripts rather than writing their own, but unlike the early mystery plays, they no longer look to the Bible for inspiration. They often have venues in which they perform regularly, although some do perform in outdoor venues or tour the show both indoors and out.

Using effects outdoors

Companies sometimes use devices such as cranes, motor vehicles, motorboats, trucks and scaffolding to create the desired effect on stage. Although these effects can be stunning they can also be extremely costly and are therefore not within the reach of smaller theatre companies. They are sometimes used gratuitously, without much thought about the relevance to the piece as a whole. In the same way that a company may try to let the setting do all the work, some companies use spectacular special effects that take precedence over the dramatic content.

Whereas indoor theatre can utilize technology to create dramatic effect, outdoor theatre can use scale, fire, water and pyrotechnics much more safely. Puppetry is often employed when creating an outdoor performance because of its dramatic effects. For example, huge puppets can suddenly loom into sight, be wheeled or carried on, or magically appear in a puff of smoke. Stories of myths and legends, which often use spectacular dramatic effects, are popular outdoor theatre themes. It is often the ingenuity involved in creating characters, sets or props out of simple techniques and in difficult environments that audiences truly appreciate.

3 WHO PUTS THE SHOW TOGETHER?

The people required to create an outdoor theatre piece do not differ greatly from the people needed to create a piece of theatre indoors. However, depending on the type of outdoor performance, the skills or experience of those in the cast and production team may vary considerably. A relatively small show can be created by just a handful of individuals who cross the divide from one skill to another with ease. Conversely, larger outdoor theatre productions that rely on special effects will need to employ specialists in each area to realize their ambitions safely and effectively. The initial budget for a show will give companies an idea of whom they can realistically employ and, consequently, the type of show that can be achieved.

THE MANAGEMENT TEAM

The producer

In most theatre companies, an administrator or a general manager (also known as a production manager) manages the business side of the production while the artistic director oversees the artistic vision. In a small company however, there may be a producer, who is responsible for overseeing all aspects of mounting a production, both technical and artistic. Conversely, in larger theatre companies there may be a range of roles required to

'There are just the six actors and me. I do FOH and stage managing. We can't afford anyone else. We hope things will get better and we can employ a stage manager next year. We have a lot of volunteer help, mainly for promotion and FOH, often from the communities we visit (who look after us, put us up over night, feed us, etc).'

(Pete Talbot,
The Rude Mechanical Theatre Company)

mount a production including a producer, general manager, managing director, production manager, administrator and artistic director.

The presence of a producer is also dependent on the type of show that is being produced. For example, a theatre show that has been commissioned by a local authority (and therefore locally funded), will have much of the administration already taken care of and may not require a producer. Some theatre shows however, are the brainchild of the producer, who will take all the initial steps to secure funding and see his/her artistic vision through to the end.

In this case, the producer will usually find both the play, or playwright, and the director to realize his/her creative goal. The producer may also be responsible for funding the project, either through his/her own company, by taking on investors or applying for funding. The producer is sometimes involved in casting or at the very least will give casting approval. He/she may coordinate production meetings, facilitate communication between departments and keep up to date on all developments from the production's first inception to the end of the project.

In larger theatre companies, the producer will liaise with agents to find the cast, negotiate with unions if required and obtain liability and workers' compensation insurance. He/she will work with the director and the playwright, if there is one, to find other technical and creative staff. Some outdoor theatre venues already have in-house staff, whom the producer will be required to hire along with the venue itself.

The general manager or administrator

Most theatre companies delegate the business side of a production to either a general manager or an administrator. In the absence of a producer, the general manager or administrator will be responsible for the overall management of all administrative aspects of putting on a show: sourcing revenue through grant applications, sponsorships or other means; negotiating contracts with staff and employees and allocating budgets to each department. The general manager or administrator will supervise the marketing for the show, the setting up and running of the box office and any fundraising activities. He/she will also deal with all legal matters, including insurance. The general manager or administrator will work with the artistic director to ensure the successful outcome of a project, and, if applicable, may report to, and work with, the company's board of directors.

THE CREATIVE TEAM

The artistic director

The artistic director brings knowledge and experience as the leader of a theatre company. The artistic director is responsible for creating an artistic vision not only for any show he/she directs, but also for any show produced under the company's name. He/she will select both the play and the director, help to organize auditions or casting and, in consultation with the show's director, put together the creative team. The artistic director is responsible for either commissioning a playwright to create a new play or coordinating workshops to devise the show. Together with the administrative staff, the artistic director will plan the company's overall artistic activities, including any educational and community work.

A festival, non-profit or amateur organization will, in most cases, have a managing director, while the creative decisions will fall to the artistic director. In theatres where there is no managing director, the artistic director often takes on the title of producing artistic director or managing artistic director to indicate his/her higher level of responsibility.

The director

Some directors are also artistic directors and so have the opportunity to select the script and creative team. The director oversees auditions, casts the company and, in consultation with the artistic director or producer, may help to select the creative team. The director decides on the interpretation of the script, or works with the writer to achieve a combined vision. The director is responsible for the overall style of the show and, ideally, should successfully bring all the elements of the show together into a coherent piece of theatre.

It falls to the director to sort out random ideas into a working throughline, sometimes referred to as the 'spine' of the play or

Director Kenneth Kimber distributing notes to the community cast of **The Princess, the Palace and the Ice Cold Bath.** *(Photo: Chris Sage)*

Stanislavski's 'superobjective'. The director will draw connections and give theatrical life to those ideas that best serve the purpose of the performance within the play's structure. The director has overall responsibility for a stage production, so must interpret the work into a theatrical event. This means rehearsing with the actors and coordinating with designers regarding the overall look, feel and practicalities of the space.

In the 1960s, directors such as Peter Brook introduced the notion that the director should collaborate with the actors and designers, rather than tell them what to do. This involves the pooling of ideas in order to get a more creative and balanced production. The organic nature of outdoor theatre lends itself to this style of directing more than to the authoritarian approach, and many companies that work exclusively on site-specific or outdoor productions work in this way.

'The ability to achieve clarity is important, as is the wit to invent elegant theatre that engages the imagination of the audience.'

(Jonathan Petherbridge, London Bubble Theatre Company)

41

Directors often work with designers and other production staff to realize their vision of the production. If they've worked together previously, they will have established a recognizable common language. A director is normally known for a particular style or genre of work, as is a designer. As a result, a successful collaboration between director and designer is something both parties are often keen to repeat. A director/designer team often remains working together for years because of this reason.

In smaller theatre companies, the director sometimes takes on the roles of producer and designer for financial reasons. This isn't an ideal working method as a single-minded vision can prevail, which consequently goes unchallenged. The skills of other theatre practitioners, for example a designer or producer, are very different from those of a director, and it's highly unlikely that one person can fulfil each role effectively.

The writer

A writer will be hired if there is no established text or if the cast and director devise the show. The writer will either create a script or work with the company through a determined period and write a script from those ideas. In the latter case, the writer will take the strongest ideas from the company and combine them with his/her own findings and research to create a script.

Alternatively, a writer may write a new play and then approach producers or theatre companies to stage the show. A playwright will often want to work with the director to make sure that his/her ideas are being communicated effectively or to make amendments to the script during rehearsals. Because of the physical nature of outdoor theatre, the relationship between the writer, director and designers becomes even more important as visual means are sometimes employed to communicate ideas, rather the spoken word. In community

plays a 'steering committee' may be set up to research ideas or stories about the area where the play is to take place. This research, along with the playwright's own findings (and possibly workshops with the cast), will form the basis of the play.

The choreographer

The choreographer is responsible to the director for the creation of all dance and movement for the production. The choreographer has a range of roles including overseeing dance rehearsals (in co-operation with the director and the stage manager), holding auditions and, even, assisting the director in casting. The choreographer may be asked to block and direct scenes in the play that move into and out of any dance numbers, as appropriate.

The designer

As for an indoor performance, an outdoor theatre piece may have a designer who designs the entire production. Alternatively, a show may have a separate designer for each specialism. In Europe and Australia especially, there is often no separation of skills, and the designer may be responsible for costume, lighting, set, sound and any mask or puppetry work. If this is the case, the role is often referred to as theatre designer, scenographer or production designer.

However, it is rare to find a designer who designs all disciplines effectively. It is much more common for designers to be concerned with just one or two linked elements: set and costume, costume and puppetry/masks; or set and lighting. Larger productions are more likely to need separate designers for each specialism. The designers work very closely with the director (and each other) to form a coherent understanding of the piece as a whole. They then create an environment in keeping with the concept and style or period of the show. All the designed elements should work

The design and making workshop at The International Festival of the Sea, where the production team, designers and crew were housed. Designs can be seen pinned to the walls as reference for the production. (Photo: Julia Knight)

together to fulfil the director's vision and concept of the piece.

The set designer

The set or stage designer is responsible for the physical appearance of the 'stage' or performance area, both in artistic and practical terms. The set designer creates a design concept and set that mirror the director's artistic vision, and takes into account the available space and budget.

In regard to outdoor theatre, the set designer's job differs tremendously from the requirements of indoor theatre. The designer must take into account the 'set' that already exists. As previously mentioned, the site will often have been chosen for its innate dynamics, so the set design may be minimal or completely redundant. In contrast, the company may have decided that the set should conflict with the site in order to achieve a specific effect or to make a statement. In this instance, the set design may become a larger undertaking.

The set designer of an outdoor theatre event will often have to come up with ingenious ideas as there is rarely the luxury of wing space, flying bars and the use of trucks or revolves. To begin with, the set designer will often create a model or at least the elements of a design that easily communicates the final set pieces. This will enable the designer to 'play' with ideas, gauge how elements might work in the environment and come up with practical solutions to scene changes. A 'model box' is also used as a tool to communicate ideas to a director. The model box helps the director understand the visual effects and to work out the practicality of entrances and exits. The designer will also create a set of accurate technical drawings in order to communicate effectively ideas to the carpenters, painters and props department.

Some designers now use CAD (Computer Aided Design) software to create their set designs, which allows other members of the company to view it as a three-dimensional image. This is still quite rare in outdoor theatre, as the 'setting' cannot be accurately manipulated in the same way as an indoor venue. However, CAD does have its uses in outdoor theatre as it shows the technical considerations of certain set pieces and gives the set-makers accurate and detailed images from which to work.

The costume designer

The costume designer is responsible for clothing all the actors from head to toe. This

The Artist and the Mariner *at the Minack Theatre, Cornwall, 2007. An ingenious design by Matt Strange, which brilliantly utilizes both the setting and the performers.* (Photo: Keith Orton)

Five Get Famous *by The Rude Mechanical Theatre Company, performed in 2007. The photo shows the strong costume design, which clearly identifies the characters.*

includes the design of wigs, hairstyles, jewellery, footwear, hats, headdresses, undergarments, swords, umbrellas, fans and unusual forms or contortions of a body shape, for example a fat suit, required by the performance. Costume designers work with the director to create costumes that are functional, affordable and imaginative. They must also take into account the activity, safety and comfort of the actors.

A costume designer seeks to enhance a character's persona within the framework of the director's vision through the costume that the character wears. He/she also works closely with the other designers to make sure that all the design elements work together and that all parties understand their responsibilities. For instance, handheld props are sometimes overlooked as they could fall into the set, costume or stage manager's domain. Anything that is designed as part of the costume will normally be the responsibility of the costume designer.

To begin with, the costume designer creates colour sketches that easily communicate the final look, and these are then presented to the director for approval. In smaller companies, where a supervisor or assistant is not present, the costume designer is responsible for the collection of costume pieces that are purchased, borrowed or constructed. A costume designer for an outdoor theatre show will need to be aware of practicalities such as potentially uneven flooring or the effects of the weather on fabrics. They also need to think about strong visuals to help an audience immediately 'read' a character from a distance or when dialogue either doesn't exist or is lost.

The composer or sound designer
The composer or sound designer interprets and emphasises themes and ideas through music and sound. He/she is responsible for planning, designing and creating soundtracks, sound effects, soundscapes, pre-show and

intermission music. All his/her work has to support the director's vision and take into account budgets and equipment limitations. The composer or sound designer may also help the director to select music that helps to bridge scene changes or transitions.

Having original music created by a composer is a luxury for any production, although it's not always affordable, or even necessary, for some companies. The hiring of a composer, as opposed to a sound designer, means the original music will necessitate the use of musicians, either during the show or to record the music beforehand.

In the technical rehearsal, the sound designer fine-tunes and sets the timing and levels of sound cues in consultation with the director, the stage manager and technical director. Most often, pre-recorded sounds or music specially created to enhance the theme and feel of the piece is used. Sound designers are important to outdoor theatre, as they are able to transform quickly the setting or inform the audience of another setting without having to move the scenery.

The sound designer also has a technical role to play in the setting up and positioning of speakers and the use of microphones. This decision, which can have a profound effect on the viewing of the piece as a whole and on the acting style, needs to be made early on in the design and rehearsal process. While it is preferable to be able to hear every word spoken, it can also be quite odd in outdoor venues to see actors in the distance while hearing their voices coming from stage left and right. An audience has grown accustomed to this in an enclosed theatre setting, but it can have an alienating, almost surreal effect in an outdoor setting. Factors that need to be taken into account here are budget restraints, the importance of the dialogue, size of the stage, actors' vocal ability and expected audience.

'You're always incredibly frightened that you won't be heard, that you'll have to shout your way through a performance, that you'll lose all the intimacy that you've rehearsed. You have to do a lot more vocal warm-ups and look after yourself, more like an opera singer than an actor. You're constantly aware of your audience, if they're bored, you know they're bored and if they're enjoying it you can see that too.'

(Sarah Woodward, actress at the Globe Theatre, London)

The lighting designer

The lighting designer is responsible for all the lighting needs of a production and works closely with the other members of the team to help create the show's overall look. He/she needs to bear in mind the limitations of the available equipment, safety restrictions and budget. In an outdoor performance, a lighting designer may only be required if the show time runs into dusk or darkness.

As with the other designers, the lighting designer is involved in the process from the start. He/she will read scripts, have production meetings and discuss the colours and effects that need to be achieved. In consultation with the director, other designers, the production manager and technical director, the lighting designer assesses the lighting requirements and then creates a lighting plot and a rough cue-by-cue lighting plan. The lighting designer generally communicates his/her ideas through storyboarding, or sketches and written text. A 'light box' is sometimes used, in conjunction with the set designer's model box, to show the director a scaled-down version of the lighting states and their effect on the set and surroundings.

Some designers use computer-generated images (CGI), which allows the lighting plot to

Andrew Derrington focuses lights for a production of The Persians *by Thiasos Theatre Company, Cyprus 2006. (Photo: Peter Barrett)*

be entered into visualization software, showing the ground plan and set design. The lighting designer can then use actual lights from the plot to demonstrate the effects on the stage of the various lighting states including gobos, colours, focus and beam angles. This technology, along with computer-aided design software, works well in established theatres that have large budgets and an array of in-house technical equipment. However, in outdoor theatre, the lack of such assets and the uncertainty of weather conditions dictate a more organic approach to design, which often relies more on robust simplicity.

In smaller theatre companies, the lighting designer may also be the technician responsible for hanging, circuiting and patching lighting units, and programming and running the light board. In larger companies, this is done by the lighting crew and operator. An established outdoor theatre venue, such as Regents Park in London, will already have a lighting rig in place and a variety of lanterns will be available for the designer to use. In a production touring to non-established venues, the company will have to take its own lighting. In

the technical rehearsal (sometimes referred to as 'cue to cue'), the lighting designer fine-tunes and sets the timing and intensities of lighting cues. The stage manager then takes over the calling of cues for the lighting board operator to follow.

The cast

The actor, performer or cast member is by far the most visible person in the theatre. Performers combine their own interpretation of a character with the artistic vision of the director to communicate the words and ideas on stage. The cast of an outdoor theatre show can range from traditional actors to performers with multi-disciplinary skills and techniques. Directors often use performers with circus, mime, dance or puppetry skills as these communicate particularly well outdoors.

Directors may sometimes require performers to be involved with the devising of the show and therefore want good 'all-rounders' with the ability to come up with ideas, teach skills and workshop ideas. All performers are responsible to the stage manager concerning their conduct backstage, the maintenance of

47

> 'At the early stage we work with a team of actors, composer, designer, director, writer, but they all work on everything within a workshop situation. After storyboarding people revert to their specialisms. As we go into more orthodox rehearsals so we employ a crack team of makers and technicians. A crew including "site captains" then installs the promenade show in each location, looking at the creative opportunities available.'
>
> (Jonathan Petherbridge,
> London Bubble Company)

the dressing room and handling of make-up, props and costumes. A touring outdoor theatre show often requires performers to be part of the crew and help with the 'get in' and 'get out', i.e. when the production is installed and when it is all removed.

THE TECHNICAL TEAM

The production manager and technical director

The technical director is responsible to the producer or production manager for the organizing and costing of the technical needs of the show. The technical director may have a wide range of responsibilities, such as directing the crew, coordinating the lighting and sound technicians and managing the set builders. It is his/her job to maintain a schedule in order to meet the deadlines of the production. He/she also works with the designers and technicians to make sure the technical rehearsals work smoothly up to the opening night.

The role of the production manager is to ensure that the production is ready for its first performance, is on schedule and within budget. They will plan, budget, coordinate and physically oversee the entire production. The

Cast of Thiasos Theatre Company rehearsing **The Persians** *in Paphos, Cyprus 2006.*
(Photo: Andrew Derrington)

production manager has a host of responsibilities and, depending on the nature of the show, may have to provide materials for the set, lights, sound, equipment rentals, special effects, staging, tents or marquees, portable toilets if necessary and emergency and car park lighting.

It is the production manager's job to provide risk assessments for each element of the performance and to complete a comprehensive 'safety and emergency plan'. He/she also has to make sure that there are qualified individuals to carry out each risk assessment and that anyone employed to install elements that might prove a risk to the general public are fully competent. He/she will then write up an on-site production schedule, making sure it is circulated to all contractors and relevant departments. In many small-scale productions, the roles of production manager and technical director are merged into one.

The stage manager

The stage manager is responsible for the smooth running of both the rehearsals and the performances. During rehearsals, the stage manager works closely with the director and communicates any notes they have made to the producer and production team. Actors always report to the stage manager, both during rehearsal and the run of the show. The stage manager also maintains a 'prompt book' that includes all the necessary information involved in the running of the show. The prompt book will have information on an actor's moves, changes to dialogue/moves/set requirements, cueing for technicians, blocking notes, schedules and all production memos and company lists.

The stage manager also liaises with the various designers and is responsible for arranging fittings with the costume designer for any costumes, wigs, hair and make-up. The stage manager has to ensure that the props and equipment are maintained and budgeted for. This may involve the procuring of props, furniture and set dressing under the set designer's guidance for use in rehearsals. Once the show has started, the stage manager oversees all backstage activities and ensures the show is technically sound and running smoothly. Sometimes there will also be a deputy stage manager and an assistant stage manager.

In smaller companies or touring shows, the stage manager may handle all areas of production. His/her role could include the organizing (and coordination) of the rehearsal schedule and performances, plus liaising with the director, technical staff and other members of stage management personnel. Other responsibilities may consist of distributing information to all departments, supervising the get in and get out, calling actors and coordinating with staff at other performance venues.

Because of the potential for technical problems arising from adverse weather conditions or other unforeseen circumstances, it's critical that a member of the stage management team calls the show, i.e. lets each actor know when he/she is required to be on stage. In the event of sudden changes, this means the stage manager will inform the performers and technical team how to proceed. Ideally, this person should be experienced in outdoor theatre and all technical aspects of health and safety, because if something were to go wrong, the entire company has to rely on them to make the most appropriate decision.

Other technical staff

* *Lighting technician/operator:* helps to rig the lights, work the dimmer board during the show, tours with the company if necessary and maintains the safety of the equipment during the run.
* *Make-up artist:* creates any make-up effects needed for the show.

49

'What I want in collaboration is the combined ideas of different elements. The input of different individuals in their roles as researcher, actor, designer, writer, director, musician should blend into a coherent whole. It's this that makes community plays thrilling. Each individual has his/her own style but neither one needs negate the other. The trick is attempting to discover where they meet in degree. The most important part is in the choice of writer, designers, musicians and community; a team who have the best chance of complementing and producing something new from what any one of those individuals could create alone.'

(Jon Oram, artistic director, Claque Theatre Company)

Technical crew, theatre staff, director and performers all discuss the 'get in' of the show **Merlin's Child** *at the Minack Theatre, 2006.* (Photo: Keith Orton)

* *Props department:* makes any props required for the show and if appropriate, maintains them during the run.
* *Scenic artist or scenic painter:* interprets the scenic elements of the set design, either as large 'flats' or as specialized painting techniques to create effects.
* *Sound technician:* works with the sound designer to cue sound into the show, tours with the company to maintain the sound equipment and works the sound board during the show.
* *Wardrobe team:* makes sure the costumes are maintained to a high standard and are clean and ready to be worn in time for each show.

Administrative Staff

* *Accountant or bookkeeper:* undertakes all matters of banking, budgeting, cash flow, contracts, financial reporting procedures and ticketing operations.
* *Box office manager:* responsible for running the box office in advance of the show and at the venue, making sure that members of staff are fully briefed as to the content of the play, duration and intervals.
* *Front of house staff and ushers:* look after the welfare of audience members and see to their needs regarding health and safety or the site and facilities. These may also include caterers and bar staff.
* *Fundraiser or development director:* implements all the fundraising activities undertaken by the company, including sponsorship and applying for grants.
* *Marketing director:* responsible for the overall image of the organization and coordinates staff and activities in all areas of education, group sales, publicity, media relations, advertising, marketing and subscriptions.

* *Publicist:* responsible for attracting the media to promote and attract people to the show, and produces posters, brochures, postcards, flyers and advertisements to draw an audience.

OTHER ROLES

* *Puppet makers:* necessary if specialized puppets are to be used in the show.
* *Education and outreach coordinators:* necessary if the company chooses to visit local schools and community groups.
* *Designer or artist:* to design flyers, programmes and merchandise.
* *Photographer:* to take photographs for publicity and archive material.
* *Voice coach:* may be required by performers to help them deal with the outdoor conditions or any accents that may be necessary.
* *Fight director:* may be required if a fight is to take place as part of the play or if battle scenes are involved.

* *Pyrotechnic specialist:* required if fire or explosive effects are taking place.
* *Water effects specialist:* coordinates effects and oversees the safe hire, use and implementation of the equipment.
* *Musicians:* may be required to record music for the show beforehand or to play live during the show.
* *Security guards:* needed if any expensive set elements, including lighting and sound equipment, are left unsecured for periods of time or overnight.

Depending on the specific requirements of the show, it is inevitable that certain staff will be needed to fulfil specific roles within the company. It is therefore very important to decide early on in the process how many members of staff are needed in order to budget accordingly. And, while certain jobs can be filled by willing volunteers, others must be carried out by people with experience in order to secure the safety of all involved.

Puppet-maker creating a puppet to be used in the performance of **The Spirit of Shivarre,** *1990. A Colway Theatre Trust community play for the Eramosa township in Ontario, Canada. (Photo: Jon Oram)*

4 THE DESIGN AND THE SPACE

There are two ways to approach an outdoor theatre show. Some companies tour each season to different venues or 'spaces' with a new or established text. Other companies, however, choose their space or 'site' first and create a piece specifically to be performed there.

I now wish to illustrate the differences between these two approaches. This will outline some of the positive and negative attributes and show potential solutions to some of the problems that arise. I will start by looking at the stimulus or starting point of two performances of which I have firsthand knowledge. This should demonstrate how the initial stimulus affected the working practice of the show and, ultimately, its outcome.

TWO PERFORMANCES

In 2006, I designed the sets and costumes for two very different outdoor theatre shows. One of the performances was a large-scale community theatre event split over two sites, entitled *The Princess, the Palace and the Ice Cold Bath*, and the other was a small-scale touring show, *The Persians*. Although both the performances were classic forms of outdoor theatre, each successfully employed different theatrical elements that were appropriate to the environment and audience. However, their approach, design and final outcome varied enormously.

The Princess, the Palace and the Ice Cold Bath

The first show, entitled *The Princess, the Palace and the Ice Cold Bath*, was performed at Claremont in 2006. Hundreds of people were involved in its production, which included a cast of almost 150 people. The project was undertaken by the Claremont Fan Court School to illustrate the history of the building and the adjacent National Trust Park. The intention was threefold: to make the area known as a historic site, to launch an education programme and to reach out to the local community.

The event took years of planning by dedicated members of staff at the school. Funds were raised through the local community and both sites – building and park – were researched extensively. A professional writer was then employed to turn this research into a large-scale theatre piece. The impetus for this performance was the history of the site so it was therefore a 'site-specific' piece of outdoor theatre.

The play set out to dramatize the history of the site where the performance was taking place. It was partly a promenade performance, in that the first half of the play was performed in the National Trust Park. The first half took place on an old grass amphitheatre with a huge lake as backdrop to the action. The audience were then moved in the interval to the

The Princess, the Palace and the Ice Cold Bath

This play has its origins in the Claremont Estate in Esher, Surrey, and began in 1708 when Sir John Vanbrugh, architect and Restoration playwright, built the first mansion on the estate. The story takes us through the various events and changes of ownership of the land, and the owners' effect on the local community. The house was sold to Thomas Pelham, later the Duke of Newcastle, in the early eighteenth century and was subsequently bought by Lord Clive, better known as 'Clive of India', who had the building demolished. He commissioned 'Capability Brown', the famous architect of the late eighteenth century, to build a new house. After Lord Clive's dramatic death, the Estate passed to several owners before being chosen by Prince Regent's newly married daughter Princess Charlotte and her husband Prince Leopold of Saxe Coburg. A reportedly bungled childbirth resulted in the death of both Charlotte and her unborn child, who would have been heir to the throne. After Charlotte's death, the Duke of Kent was ordered, for the sake of the succession, to marry the widowed sister of Leopold, who gave birth to Victoria. However, Claremont remained the property of Victoria's uncle, Prince Leopold, who invited the family of King Louis Philippe to stay there after its exile from France during the French revolution of 1848. The young Queen Victoria spent much of her childhood at Claremont and purchased the property on Leopold's death for her youngest son Leopold, Duke of Albany. In 1922, Claremont was confiscated from the royal family and underwent many changes and divisions. In 1931, the building and thirty-three acres of land became a school for girls, but in 1940 the site was evacuated, and the building, now covered in camouflage net, was taken over by Hawker Aircraft Ltd. The building was later returned to the school and the grounds became National Trust property, which they still are today.

View from the seating in the amphitheatre during the production of The Princess, the Palace and the Ice Cold Bath, *Claremont, Surrey, 2006.*

View from the audience towards the mansion house, which acted as the backdrop to the second half of the play, The Princess, The Palace and the Ice Cold Bath, *Surrey, 2006.*

second site, which utilized the steps and foreground of a historic mansion house. The first half of the play was seen by an audience looking down at the action and in broad daylight. The second half was witnessed either at the same level or looking up at the action and at twilight, which then descended into semi-darkness.

The Persians

The second show that I worked on was an adaptation of Aeschylus' Persians, created by an established theatre company called Thiasos Theatre Company. It involved eight actors,

three musicians and a minimal set. It would be touring to three amphitheatres in Cyprus and an outdoor venue in Oxford. The Company is well known for its English translations and adaptations of ancient Greek plays and for upholding an ancient tradition in modern times. It seeks to remain true, in translation, to the original script and puts a huge amount of research into how the plays might have originally been performed.

The show rehearsed and premiered in a church in London before going to Cyprus and then returning to an outdoor venue in Oxford. The company adapted each venue on the tour

The Persians opens with the chorus, representing Persian Elders and Queen Atossa, awaiting news of her son King Xerxes' expedition against the Greeks. A messenger arrives, bringing news of defeat and delivers the names of the Persian leaders killed in battle. He then reveals that King Xerxes escaped and is on his way home.

The Queen, seeking consolation, visits the tomb of her dead husband, Darius. He appears as a ghost, and tells her that the Persians were defeated because of the folly of their son, Xerxes, who constructed a bridge of boats across the sea and by doing so offended the gods.

Xerxes later returns. Defeated and ashamed, he is unaware that his own actions were the cause of defeat. At the end of the play, which is filled with lamentations by Xerxes and the chorus, the Queen re-crowns him King.

to the needs of the show and, consequently, adapted the show to the constraints or strengths of each venue. This type of show could be described as 'touring', although there is also an element of 'site generic' in that the three amphitheatres had similar qualities, and the show had been designed and directed with these fundamental qualities in mind.

The creative teams, cast and crew

The cast and crew necessary for each production also differed tremendously. The show at Claremont was a huge undertaking by people who were passionate about their aims, but had never staged something of this size before. To help the production succeed, they took the decision early on to employ professional advisers and specialist practitioners in various areas. Because of this, an unusually large number of people were involved. In contrast, Thiasos had worked for years producing shows, and the significantly smaller size of its production meant that relatively few people were involved.

Getting started, Claremont

Auditions for the community play were held in an all-inclusive manner. Anybody who wanted to take part, either from the school or the local community, was given a role to play. The cast quickly swelled to 150 people, and they subsequently got involved in role-play and improvisation early on. The writer of the play, Rib Davies, was involved with these improvisation workshops and based a large amount of the play's final content on these sessions.

The Persians *by Thiasos Theatre Company performing an 'open dress' inside a church in Hampstead, London, before setting off to Cyprus.*

55

The play included specific scenes where large groups of people could inhabit the stage at the same time, allowing every participant some sort of role. The play was also written with varying age groups in mind to accommodate the participants' vast differences in age. Although the decision had been made early on in the process to employ professional practitioners such as a writer, director, lighting designer, songwriter, set and costume designer, many other tasks were undertaken by volunteers from the school and community.

These tasks were essential to the success of the venture. It was a huge undertaking, so the project required volunteers at every step: from licensing, fundraising and finding sponsorship to the box office, security and stewarding. The task of returning the site to its original state afterwards also had to be considered. Although not directly part of the creative performance, these jobs had to be allocated and considerably increased the number of those involved.

By contrast, an established outdoor venue has the staff to take care of these considerations. A touring theatre company may also have the necessary staff, but if the intention is to tour to non-established venues, or to choose a 'site' that ordinarily doesn't host theatre productions, then all these jobs need to be considered.

Getting started, Thiasos

Thiasos Theatre Company began by holding auditions for each member of the cast and musicians and employed a stage manager, choreographer, director, designer and musical director. Unlike for the Claremont play, its starting point was an established script. However, this script needed to be interpreted by the team in order to produce a coherent dynamic. An idea of the look and feel of the show was established before rehearsals started, and the creative team then worked with the performers to solve issues arising in rehearsal.

Keeping community cast members occupied with painting set pieces during the long, all-day rehearsals.
(Photo: Chris Sage)

Outdoor considerations

Huge variants existed between the two shows regarding the weather. The Claremont play was designed to be performed in the potentially wet English summer, involved grassy settings and moved from daylight to twilight through the course of the show. The play by Thiasos was designed to be performed in the sun, during an almost guaranteed balmy evening, with stone as the stage surface.

The challenges at Claremont

The comfort of the cast, especially of the very young or elderly members, was most important at Claremont since so many people – and of different ages – were involved. But because cast members were largely inexperienced, long

rehearsals *in situ* were inevitable. The performers needed time to get used to the space, the exits and entrances, and to learn to project their voices. Consequently, all-day outdoor rehearsals were commonplace.

Because of the unpredictable British weather, these rehearsals were either rained upon, causing the grass to be muddy, or stifling, as the sun beat down. There were no areas for shelter during the rehearsal period so the cast had to be prepared with sun cream, water, Wellington boots, umbrellas and extra layers of clothing. I requested that cast members should have their own flat, sensible shoes to wear, rather than hiring period shoes for them. I also requested they wear these shoes throughout rehearsals so they could become

Marquee hired for the show at Claremont to act as dressing room and holding area for the cast before and during Act 1. (Photo: Chris Sage)

57

Paphos amphitheatre in Cyprus. One of the venues used by Thiasos Theatre Company, 2006.
(Photo: Andrew Derrington)

accustomed to the different surfaces and find out any potential risks well in advance. Taking cast members' welfare into consideration during the show was more difficult as they needed to stay in their costumes. However, they were only in their costumes for the time they were on stage, and there was a covered holding area for them to change in or to take shelter in between scenes.

Because of the transition into evening, the show at Claremont also required lighting during the performance. This was another potential hazard since the community cast was neither used to wearing costumes nor experienced in performing under stage lights. So we made sure the edges of the stage were clearly marked, and rehearsals were in costume and on set, early on in the process. We also gave priority to cast members who had large costumes or particularly quick changes to make.

The challenges for Thiasos
Regarding weather conditions, the biggest challenge for the show in Cyprus was the potential for sunstroke and dehydration. The show had a largely British cast, who were not used to working in high, Mediterranean temperatures. The cast also had very limited time to rehearse in these conditions and to acclimatize to the set and the environment. Unlike the show at Claremont, the cast had rehearsed in a studio in London with only two days onsite rehearsal at the first venue in Cyprus.

The different setting had obvious challenges cast members hadn't encountered in England. Their singing as a chorus completely altered once they were in an outdoor setting, and the feeling of hot stone underfoot was totally different from the cool rehearsal space. They also had the challenge of vast space and playing to an audience of an amphitheatre. This transition from indoors to outdoors can sometimes throw less experienced performers, but the cast, all professional actors, coped with this transition quite quickly.

DESIGN CONSIDERATIONS

Although the Claremont show and the Thiasos performance differed in scope and scale, there were some commonalities regarding the design solutions. Each piece needed to be approached with a completely fresh look at the practicalities and the aesthetics of designing for a show outdoors.

Designing for Claremont

With a cast of 150 people and roughly 600 characters, plus a fairly restrained budget, my challenge was to work out how to costume large groups of characters in various period settings.

Three major factors to consider were:

* *Keeping the audience focused.* The site(s) had huge stages with the sky, lakes, buildings and views that could easily distract attention from the action. The costumes and set had to keep the audience focused whilst making them aware of who the characters were.
* *Keeping the audience informed of where and when the action was taking place.* The play was written with about eight different time periods, dating from the 1720s right up to the present day. At times the stage was inhabited with characters from different time periods and to make matters even more difficult, they would also converse with each other.
* *Making the scene and costume changes as quick as possible.* It was important that the transitions would run fluidly, without the possibility of having curtains dropping or stages revolving to make these transitions. Also,

there were no wings for the cast to disappear into to make quick changes with dressers on hand to assist.

Like many plays, we moved from winter to summer, indoor settings to outdoors and from land to sea. This all took place in the same space and under the setting sun of an August day. To alleviate some of the challenges thrown up by the script and the site, I decided to allocate a colour to each time period, so the audience would instantly recognize characters that 'belonged' together or to a scene. I hoped this would alert the audience or refocus attention each time the stage washed with a new colour.

Cast members from the same 'time period' performing in **The Princess, the Palace and the Ice Cold Bath.** *(Photo: Kim Stapff)*

59

Supporting the story

The costumes changed dramatically during the performance, and the overall body silhouettes of both men and women took different shapes throughout the production. To give the audience no doubt as to which time in history each scene or group of characters belonged, I took the most iconic shape of each period and exaggerated it slightly. This overstated way of designing each costume would help to 'place' the character. I also played with the historical accuracy of each period by exaggerating skirt widths, hat shapes etc. Without the focus of lighting (as in an indoor venue), this would create an impact on stage and help the audience to follow the action.

A basic dress code

Although I had 150 cast members, the writer had written many more characters and the total rose to more than 600 changes in costume. Not all of these were main characters: most were part of a group. As a response to the high number of cast and costume changes, I gave each actor a 'basic' dress code: white chemise and long white petticoat for the females,

and white shirt with neutral coloured breeches for the males. I designed all the costumes around the convention that the performers would dress in the appropriate colour and style, but this would be worn over the 'basic' costume to alleviate the need for a full costume change. This design solution in turn helped with the quick changes required – some performers had as many as six characters to play – and also to keep the budget on target.

Budgetary requirements made it necessary to have only the one 'holding area' for all the performers – men, women and children. The design solution alleviated the need to hire another marquee as none of the cast members needed to change completely in front of each other. Their 'basic' undergarments, made of lightweight cotton, performed another function by providing a layer of material next to the skin that was effective for staying cool in the hot weather and an extra layer of warmth on the cold days or if the temperature dropped in the evening.

Identifying the characters

Unless a performer was playing an extremely

The gardeners wear a brown or green apron on top of their 'basic' costume simply to denote their character. (Photo: Kim Stapff)

French revolutionaries, recognized by their berets and the tricolour flag.

iconic character – one who had to be immediately recognizable for the historical integrity of the play – I gave the characters just one or two items to identify them within the period. I had to choose fairly obvious icons to suggest to the audience who these characters were, and I pared the design down to the basic elements and symbols to convey a character type or profession.

Allowing for just two items to create the character, the changes would be quick and clearly signalled to the audience. Once the convention had been established, the audience would look out for the items 'describing' the character.

Here are a couple of examples of how paring down the design worked. The play started with almost every member without a specific role being cast as a gardener. I gave each gardener an apron in the allocated colour and either a hat or a tool to use. In a scene of the

French Revolution, I decided to present the cast in the tricolour colours: red, white and blue. The revolutionaries wore their 'basics' with the typical red revolutionist cap and a rosette on the side. Some of them also wore a cummerbund or sash, while others carried flags in red, white and blue. The aristocrats involved in this scene were dressed in darker shades of the same colours – navy, cream and claret red. This immediately identified them as being part of the scene, but also set them apart from the revolutionists.

Choosing the set

In response to the outdoor conditions of the two sites at Claremont and the format I had chosen for the costumes, I decided to keep the staging as simple as possible. In keeping with the design concept for the costumes, I chose just one or two symbolic pieces of set to 'describe' the scene. Using representational

61

images effectively suggested to the audience where or when the scene was taking place. It also concentrated on the function of the set design rather than on pure aesthetics.

I questioned every prop and set piece that was required by the script and the director, not only because they may have been unnecessary but also because scene changes were built into the action and executed by a non-professional cast. Each scene was quickly established with just one or two poignant pieces and, consequently, the action from one scene to the next moved rapidly. This convention also enabled the design team to concentrate on a few, well-made and well-considered items, rather than trying to fill the space with set pieces and props.

To deal with some of the practicalities involved in the show, I designed two multi-functional carts. These were to be used throughout to become the various 'sets' required for each period. These carts, with the addition of cut-out boards attached to the sides, served a variety of uses as wheelbarrows, carriages, a yacht, a ship, a bed, a luggage van and even part of a barricade. And as they were on wheels, they were also invaluable to the cast and crew for moving props, costumes and sets between the two sites.

Thinking about the space

The first half of the show was set on the grassy amphitheatre, with a lake in the background. It was decided that the show would open with the 'gardeners' positioned at a distance on the other side of the lake. By doing this, we utilized the whole space on offer and so declared the entire area our stage.

Bath scene, created by handheld, painted 'marbled' flat boards, one of which shows a stylized tap to help suggest 'bath'.

Designing for Thiasos Theatre Company

In complete contrast, *The Persians* production required just eleven costumes, a touring 'tomb' and some well-chosen props.

The three major factors to consider were:

* *How to create costumes that would focus the audience's attention and help them understand the dynamics between the characters.* With relatively few characters and a small set on stage, the costume designs had to support the other disciplines by drawing the audience's attention.
* *How to change the actors' costumes on stage.* All the chorus members needed to change costume during the course of the show. The Queen lost some of her finery at one point and one of the chorus members became the King returned from the dead. This disrobing and swapping of costume had to take place in front of the audience.
* *How to create a set and costumes that were transportable by air.* The show's set pieces had to fit within the luggage constraints of an ordinary charter plane.

HMS Leviathan, *made from a cut-out board attached to one of the carts, and complete with sailors and mast.*

Getting started

I started by focusing on the stone flooring and seating of the amphitheatres in Cyprus. The costumes were originally sketched onto tracing paper, against a card of similar colour to the stone of the performance area. This enabled me to see what the costumes might look like in the space and to better understand which colours and shapes would stand out.

Thinking about the space

As opposed to a normal set behind the actors, the stone flooring became the most considered backdrop. This was because the playing area needed to be brought as far forward on the stage as possible, and because of the construct of an amphitheatre, an audience would always be looking down at the action. So in fact, the audience would mainly view the stone ground as a backdrop to the costumes.

Identifying the characters

Before the production began, the company director, Yana Zarifi, undertook a research trip to Uzbekistan and was able to bring back fabric samples of traditional silks to choose from.

As with the show at Claremont, I 'grouped' the performers and chose designs and colours to identify them. The chorus was dressed in patterned fabrics of various colours, whereas royalty wore plain but striking full-length gowns of blue and red silks with heavy gold jewellery. Each regal costume included a lining of metallic orange silk as, in the design stage, I

Chorus members dressed in coloured and patterned Uzbekistani silk robes and hats, New College Gardens, Oxford, 2006.

discovered how alien the orange silk looked against the natural landscape. This striking use of colour would further separate the royalty from the rest of the cast. The show was spoken in English and sung in Persian so it was vital the costumes aided the audience in understanding as much as possible.

Providing suitable costumes
As with the theatre piece at Claremont, we had the technical difficulty of changing the actors' costumes on stage. There were no wings to hide in or any hope of touring a large piece of scenery for them to undress behind. It was therefore necessary to design a 'basic' outfit for the actors to wear that was entirely in keeping with the Persian style. What's more, the actors' basic outfit couldn't have too many layers or use thick material, as they remained on stage in potentially high temperatures for the duration of the show.

Using the Uzbekistani silks, the solution was to design lightweight gowns with cotton lin-

ings and hats for the actors to wear. The gowns and hats were all slightly different in shape and colour, but created a uniform pattern when grouped together. Each character had a large sash tied around the waist to keep the gown closed, which could be untied at the moment required to disrobe. The sashes were also knotted, as they would have been traditionally, without the use of modern fastenings. This kept the clothing as authentic as possible and removed the worry of any modern fastenings being seen by the audience.

Shaping the space
The Thiasos Company had rehearsed the play in an area equivalent to the smallest of the amphitheatres they were touring to. However, there was then the issue of performing in a larger venue and re-creating a stage edge for the performers. By bringing the action forward in the bigger spaces, the audience's attention would be more focused on the centre of the action, and this was achieved by simply placing

a perimeter of large candles around the back of the space to concentrate the stage area.

Placing the set

The set consisted of a few key areas: a space for the musicians; stage left, the king's gown hung upstage; and downstage, the lament area, where there was also a replica of Darius' tomb and various pots and jugs. The tomb was made in four parts so it would comply with the luggage restrictions and then painted to complement the stone of the amphitheatres in Cyprus.

Changing venues

The situation that arose when the Thiasos Company brought the show to an outdoor venue in Oxford demonstrates just how important design decisions are. The venue in Oxford had grass flooring, with stone steps located centre stage leading away from the action. In this case, the audience was situated at ground

'The Queen' and her son in plain silks with metallic orange linings, Paphos, Cyprus. 2006. (Photo: Andrew Derrington)

This photograph shows the chorus members stripped down to 'basics', New College Gardens, Oxford 2006.

level, not above as was the case in Cyprus. This venue was obviously very different from the sites the show had been designed for.

For instance, the tomb had been made and finished to replicate the stone flooring of the amphitheatres and, consequently, it didn't merge with the grass flooring it was now on. Despite this incongruent element in the set, when it transferred to Oxford, the stone steps leading away from the centre stage lent the piece a regal nature it hadn't previously had. Once again, this reinforces the idea that a great deal is learnt in the process of touring about how different sets and costumes can look depending on location.

LEFT: *A chorus member plays the part of King Darius by putting on the gown, on stage, New College Gardens, Oxford 2006.*

The 'stone' tomb of Darius, the King's gown and the various bowls on set, New College Gardens, Oxford 2006. (Photo: Andrew Derrington)

5 CHOOSING THE SPACE

I n some cases, theatre companies may be given a choice of sites in which to perform during a specific event and will choose the one that most closely fulfils their requirements. However, this chapter deals with companies that wish to find a site, or

'There are countless outdoor spaces to perform in which don't cost money (village greens, playing fields, pub fields, gardens, etc.), quite apart from heritage sites (which usually are much less financially viable). You just need to find your audience. It is much easier to organize than looking for indoor spaces (which are usually controlled by people who want their cut).

At the beginning I approached parish clerks about doing a show for the community. We only do new venues by invitation now and if it meets our criteria and can be fitted in. We like to add a few new ones every year, which means losing others that aren't going so well. We have to apply for TENs (Temporary Event Notices). I am a Personal Licence Holder and can apply for this myself. We get little funding. ACE almost always turns us down. We are supported by a few county and district councils (West Sussex County Council are our biggest funder). We get given money by rich patrons! To be honest we largely work outside the conventional theatre and arts industry.'

(Pete Talbot, artistic director,
The Rude Mechanical Theatre Company)

'When attending work in unusual spaces, an audience comes along with fewer expectations. In fact I don't think it has any expectations because there's not that unwritten contract that there is when you buy a theatre ticket. When you go to a theatre, the lights will dim and everyone knows what's going to happen.

If you go to a bridge, for example, you have no idea what's going to happen and therefore there's no unwritten contract and an audience will come with a much more open mind.

(Paul Pinson, Artistic Director,
Boilerhouse)

sites, to house their production or have been inspired by an outdoor location but need to find funding and permission to make their vision a reality. I will explore the considerations around choosing these sites and the possibilities of gaining the use of them.

MATTERS TO CONSIDER

If a company has already chosen the type of outdoor theatre it wishes to perform, it must then choose the most appropriate site to perform in. This will be based on a huge variety of criteria, which I detail below. It's exciting to note that the types of outdoor sites available to companies are becoming increasingly more dynamic.

A theatre company wanting to perform outside will first need to decide whether the show is touring, site specific, site generic, promenade or a mixture of these. The decision may obviously be linked to the initial impetus of the show or the ideology of the theatre company. But in general terms, there are some fundamental issues that should be considered on a practical level before choosing a site to perform in.

Why Shakespeare?

The vast majority of outdoor theatre seen today is either Shakespearian or children's shows aimed at a family audience. There seems to be a lack of outdoor theatre that explores new writing or devised shows that are site specific. This could be because companies are aware that audiences expect to see Shakespeare or children's classics outdoors, and if they move away from this convention, there just won't be an audience. However, there is most definitely a growing audience for new writing and site-specific productions. New outdoor companies are appearing all the time and the number of sites in which they can perform is growing rapidly.

Who is the audience?

In an outdoor performance, the audience should be considered right from the initial thinking process. In fact, the audience is almost the first consideration. Although it's stating the obvious, you need an audience to perform to, so the location needs to have a community in the vicinity. This community must also be persuaded to come and watch the show and in some cases, to become actively involved in it.

Therefore the geographical location of the space (or spaces) is the first thing to take into consideration. For example, many young families with children tend to congregate in the suburbs of large cities, while more elderly people tend to head for the coast (so putting on a children's show by the coast may not draw the audience that was anticipated). These are broad generalizations about location or groups of people, but some assumptions can be made as to the types of shows different groups may want to see. It is important that a company both identifies its target audience and establishes the presence of this audience in the local vicinity.

Placing the audience

Deciding where to put the audience is absolutely crucial because it can dramatically change the whole look and feel of the piece. The audience may be placed in the usual 'end on' formation (like an indoor theatre), but typically in outdoor theatre, the audience tends to snake around the performance area. Outdoor theatre lends itself to every conceivable positioning of an audience so when choosing where to put it, do keep an open mind. The space may open up profound opportunities for both you and the audience in regard to staging.

An audience that is forced to interact with the action, either as a promenade or simply in the space, can make for a lively and more intimate feel. However, making audience members interact within the action can also be

'The audience are no longer silent witnesses in the dark, but become a major scenic element as much in evidence as the performers. In addition to the central, shared performance space are the spaces where the theatre does its business in the foyer, box-office, bars and entrances. Outside, the car park and the route to theatre are all seen as part of the "performance environment" and potential sites for things to happen.'

(Jon Oram, Claque Theatre Company)

Creation Theatre Company's performance of A Midsummer Night's Dream, 2005.

quite intimidating for them, whereas positioning them outside the action creates a slightly more secure feeling as it will no doubt be a situation they are more accustomed to. There are no right or wrong ways of placing an audience, and both involving and distancing it from the action can work, depending on the nature of the piece.

THE SIZE OF THE SPACE

The type of theatre show may well determine the amount of space required. Many community shows, for instance, have a performing cast of at least 100 people. The size of the cast also dictates the space needed backstage to house performers when they are offstage. It's also important to bear in mind the space needed for an audience. A free theatre performance, for example one that has been paid for by a local council, will attract many more people than a paying event, so bear this in mind when estimating audience numbers.

Each site will have maximum audience capacity, and, ultimately, you should aim to be as close to capacity as possible. The two scenarios you don't want are either turning audience members away because the venue is too small, or ruining the ambiance because the venue is too big and empty. Therefore, the aesthetics and natural dynamics of the space should be carefully examined as to whether it can practically serve its purpose as both a stage and an auditorium.

Seating

The space may have a naturally raked aspect that would serve as seating, making it relatively easy for all the audience members to see the action clearly. Alternatively, it may have naturally formed stage areas that are slightly higher so that the audience looks up at the action. However, it isn't absolutely essential to have either. Audience members invariably place themselves where they have a good view – above, below or on the same level as the action – and some productions choose to put structures in place to aid the audience's view.

Whether the space might benefit from fixed seating is another possibility to consider. If the space is small, this can have real benefits as it means that the audience is required to sit close together to maximise audience capacity in the space available. However, fixed seating fundamentally alters the feel of the show because it can take away some of the interaction between the players and the audience.

Many outdoor productions require the audience to sit on the ground (or chair if one has been brought). If this is the case, they will always make the specific request that chair sitters place themselves behind the people sitting on the ground. Some companies even provide their audiences with folding out stools, especially if it is a promenade performance. If the audience is continually on the move, it is worth considering whether it needs to sit down at all. A promenade performance may require the audience to visit numerous locations, and seating, whether stationary or mobile, might be an encumbrance.

Promenade performances

The community theatre company, Claque, formerly known as Colway Theatre Trust, has a simple solution to the problem of seating and standing. Its promenade productions are invariably performed around the outside of the audience. Cast members are then placed on movable stages, which can end up being placed on all four sides of the space. The audience then turns to view the appropriate stage to see the action. In order that no elderly or disabled people are excluded from seeing the show, limited seating is also provided on one of the unmovable stages.

A participatory performance by The London Bubble Company, entitled Myths, Rituals and White Goods, *showing the semicircular audience configuration set in place by means of pre-positioned rugs and chairs.*

In contrast, a show called *Souterrain* by WildWorks Theatre Company, performed in Stamner Village as part of the Brighton Festival, was a promenade performance that took its audience on a journey for nearly two hours and provided no seating at all. The audience was herded from one 'set' to the next as part of the story and was totally included in the action. This show encompassed the whole village of Stamner and thoroughly utilized the unusually large performance space. The show also toured but involved the local community of each tour venue and therefore had a very different dynamic at each site. A show of this kind is such a unique experience, and each venue required long preparation periods to exploit fully the potential of the community and fully explore the space itself.

ACCESS TO THE SITE

Access to the site is a very important consideration, not just regarding health and safety, but also for the technical and backstage staff, and the audience. If a site is already established and regularly houses productions, then all the necessary precautions will be in place to make it as easily accessible as possible. If the chosen site isn't used for theatrical purposes, then the feasibility of access to all areas will need to be considered.

If the performance requires large staging or pieces of set, suitable transport will need to have access to the area. Anything that hinders this access, such as steps or ditches, will have to be negotiated, but it doesn't necessarily rule the space out completely as smaller loads can be carried. A company must also make sure that audience members, especially wheelchair users, are able easily to access the venue. Each borough council has an access officer who can advise companies on making their venue safe and accessible, especially in the event of an emergency.

A performer addressing the audience directly as part of WildWorks' promenade performance, Souterrain, Stamner Village, 2006.

Above and below ground

The site must allow access for emergency services. It is essential that all aspects of the site, above and below ground, are considered. The entire site, such as the structural integrity of the space, needs to be thought about early on in the process. Overlooking any important factors could lead to the show being refused permission on health and safety grounds or not having the required elements to perform. A recent outdoor production encountered transport problems for the St John's Ambulance, the scaffolding truck and the light and sound van. None of them could access the site as intended because of ancient tunnels that ran underneath the grass. The company discovered, quite late on in the production, that the tunnels couldn't be guaranteed to take the weight of the vehicles. Fortunately, the company managed to find an alternative route and the show went ahead as planned.

Access to the stage

The Minack Theatre in Cornwall is one of the most stunning outdoor theatres in the country. Unfortunately, it also has possibly the most difficult get in restrictions. The theatre is cut away into the edge of a cliff so the only access to the stage is down fifty or so uneven steep stone steps. This means any transport has to remain parked at the top of the site, while everything is carried down individually. The Minack does present wonderful opportunities for designs and sets – the backdrop is the sea – and it is easy to be tempted by these possibilities. But the practicalities of the site necessitates that every piece of set needs to be made into a size that can be safely carried.

To complicate matters, the unevenness and rake of the Minack's stage floor makes the use

'One important thing to check when considering the use of an outdoor space is the angle and contours of the stage floor, particularly if considering using movable large props or scenery. One classic oversight led to the need to re-block whole sections of a performance. A specially constructed boat, which contained several members of the cast who were steering and moving the boat with their feet, became a complete impossibility when introduced to the space. This was due to the steeper than anticipated anti-rake (there for quick drainage in wet conditions). The boat was impossible to steer and simply slid upstage until it came to rest against the back wall.'

(Keith Orton, theatre designer, talking about a performance with the Central School of Speech and Drama at the Minack Theatre)

Van unloading all the set, props and costumes to the show **The Quest** *at the Minack Theatre. (Photo: Keith Orton)*

With the van parked as near as possible to the site, this photograph demonstrates the perilous task of bringing heavy set pieces into the Minack Theatre. (Photo: Keith Orton)

ACOUSTICS AND SOUND

It is always advisable to check the acoustics of the intended space. Whether or not the show will make use of microphones may depend on the style of theatre or the vocal abilities of the performers. It's vital to remember that the sound quality will always be better without the audience present. An audience will inevitably make some noise during the performance and just its presence will soak up some of the sound.

Microphones and recorded effects

Outdoor theatre shows can work brilliantly without the use of microphones or pre-recorded effects. But of course, the desire to make the words or a dramatic statement audible may sometimes outweigh the desire for the

A production of **Merlin's Child**, *performed by students from the Central School of Speech and Drama in 2003, and designed by Keith Orton. (Photo: Keith Orton)*

of wheels almost impossible. The set of steps leading from stage left makes the actors' entrances with large props problematic too. What this demonstrates is the effect the site can have on the entire composition of a production. Therefore the difficulties of actually getting to the site, and the character of the site itself, for example flooring, steps etc., need to be considered in the very first stages of production.

intimacy and naturalistic feel of unaided speech. The careful placement of speakers is also important as the effect of surrounding sound can have an alienating effect on an outdoor audience. In an outdoor setting, watching an actor say his/her lines in front of you while hearing the words from behind can be unsettling. This could simply be because an audience is accustomed to indoor theatre, where the sound quite naturally 'bounces' from the walls. Sound, obviously, cannot be contained in an outdoor setting and the production may lose some of its naturalism.

But there is plenty of scope for using microphones and sound effects to create a specific dramatic effect. And if there are musicians, or there is recorded music, it's vital to consider the volume of the actor's speech as he/she may be required to talk over the top of the music and still be heard. When choosing an outdoor venue, the proximity of residential housing must also be considered. Each local council has guidelines governing the use of amplified sound and has the power to refuse permission for productions that do not work within them.

Ambient sound

Ambient sounds can interfere with the audience's overall acoustic level so it's advisable to check the site for sound at the exact same time as the performance, and, if possible, at a similar time of year. Ideally, the planning of the

'It's worth pointing out that Shakespeare's actors only had to cope with the noise from the local bear-baiting pit. Modern open-air shows often have to compete with an easyJet summer timetable full of noisy 747s.'

(Martin Tomms, actor, Illyria Theatre Company)

show and choosing of location is so far in advance that the production team has the chance to visit the site early on, ideally a year before, in order to ascertain any potential problems. It's also a good idea to check if any major building or transport plans such as road works, fairs or increased traffic are scheduled to commence during the performance dates.

HEALTH AND SAFETY

Matters of health and safety must be at the forefront of almost every decision, regardless of the intended size of the performance. A company should always contact the local authority for general guidance and, ideally, the fire service for advice relating to fire safety. Companies should also obtain a copy of the *Event Safety Guide*, universally referred to as the 'purple guide'. This is available in book form or published online by the government's Health and Safety Executive. It gives complete guidance on all aspects of health and safety for music and entertainment events.

It will be clear whether the site looks generally safe just by looking around it. But it is also worth creating a 'site assessment'. This should pinpoint the particular hazards of the space and also detail any possible solutions. When the site has been fully evaluated on its strengths and weaknesses, it will then be easier to make a judgement regarding its suitability.

You may find a site that's almost perfect in every respect, but has one major obstacle (for example, limited access), which means that it's simply not practical. Alternatively, it's quite common to find sites that aren't perfect overall, but can be modified to make the space work. Be realistic in your site assessment! Anything that needs doing to the site to comply with health and safety regulations will probably have budget implications. Don't just think it will work, make sure it will.

What to look out for

There are a number of factors to consider when assessing the safety of a site including the presence of open water, uneven ground and any derelict buildings in the vicinity. Because of the informal setting of outdoor theatre, it's advisable to expect the audience to behave differently from an indoor one. If there is something to climb onto to get a better view, an audience member will invariably try to do so. Likewise, if there is something in the space that can be leaned on, sat on or crawled into, check that it can withstand the treatment. Be prepared to cordon off areas if they are deemed unsafe from this type of attention. The company will also have to produce a 'risk assessment', which has to be submitted to the council in order to gain permission to stage the production.

CHOOSING A PUBLIC SPACE

In choosing a location (or locations) for a performance, the company should always take into account whether the site is open to the public at large during the rehearsals and performance. It's not always possible to get permission in a public venue to define an area that can only be entered by ticket holders. Even if a barrier or ticket booth is erected, it may not have an impact on keeping out comments or noise from the general public.

The Dong with the Luminous Nose, *a promenade performance by the* **London Bubble Theatre Company, 2007.** *(Photo: Steve Hickey)*

Inevitably with outdoor theatre, there could always be some kind of outside interference, but a company may want to control the proximity of this interference to the space. It's advisable to check the laws regarding the site before committing to it. There is also the potential of turning the possibility of outside interference to your advantage, which is a technique that the theatre company London Bubble used in its show, *The Dong with the Luminous Nose*.

As *The Dong with the Luminous Nose* began, there were loud comments from a group of teenagers who seemed to have infiltrated the audience. When told to be quiet and then asked to leave by the increasingly agitated members of the audience, one of the teenagers came forward and chased the actor from the stage. He then began his soliloquy, and the audience slowly realized that the teenagers were actually part of the action. The fact that the audience believed the teenagers to be real nuisance-makers, informs us of a situation that could very easily happen in outdoor theatre. It also displays the inherent fragility of outdoor theatre that cannot exist in quite the same way indoors.

If a theatre company is willing to perform in an open public space (for example, the promenade performance in a park by the London Bubble Theatre Company), it should be confident that the performers are adept at dealing with interference and that there are staff on the lookout for potential health and safety risks.

RESPECTING THE SITE

It is always a good idea to choose a site that, in its current state, suits your requirements as closely as possible. This will inevitably reduce the amount of work you have to do to it and helps to keep the cost down. It will also reduce the risk of running into potential problems with the site owners.

A good example of sites that offer obvious

Metamorphosis by London Bubble, 2006. The company used an old-fashioned lawnmower to denote a space craft.

benefits regarding, for example, infrastructure, period and access are buildings owned by the National Trust. The National Trust hosts many outdoor theatre shows each summer, as do a variety of stately homes and castles. However, the owners and workers at these sites are naturally protective of their space and can be less than amenable with theatre companies (or audience members) who choose not to respect the venue and its rules.

Although there are advantages in selecting a site that is better adapted to outdoor theatre, there are some points to consider. For example, if it rains the owners may restrict rehearsals because of the damage to the grass or deny access to vehicles or heavy machinery. When choosing a site that has historical significance or relies on public access for part of its income, the company must be willing to make compromises. A great deal of pain can be avoided if you are aware of what is and isn't permissible.

Check with the site's administrators before making concrete decisions about the design and use of the space. If a show cannot work properly without certain elements – for example, fireworks, horses or loud music – then make sure that the venue can accommodate them. There may also be historical or listed buildings within the site that the company has been given permission to use. This may well be an exciting opportunity, but bear in mind any damage to the building by you or the audience is chargeable. It's also worth finding out how much insurance costs before making a commitment.

The same rules apply to touring companies. Many theatre companies, especially those that spend the summer on tour, travel with a self-supporting set. They aren't dependent on structures within the site and can, almost, unfold the set and perform anywhere. However, whether the touring production takes place on private or public land, it's still a good idea to check what is and isn't allowed.

SITE SPECIFIC

The physical formation of the site, as well as its geographical location, will determine how it is 'read' by an audience. The physical formation is important when producing a site-specific piece of theatre. There are many factors that will shape the audience's response to a space: the lie of the land, the soil, the building structures on the site, the former, or existing, use of the site and the general aesthetics or physicality of the space. All of these factors should be used to inspire a company to create a piece of theatre that is truly a response to the site.

A company also has to take into account that the audience may have perceived 'memories' – or engrained ideas – of the site and these can be difficult to change. Conversely, it may be that these memories can be explored as part of the piece. 'Memories' can take the form of facts or myths surrounding the site, and the company may wish to exploit them within the space. Alternatively, the memories regarding the usual function of the site may be purposely disregarded in an attempt to give the site a false significance or a new mythology. A theatre company is completely free to try either to erase previous memories or to reuse them in a different way and ultimately create new memories.

TOURING

Each different venue on a tour can present a new set of challenges and creates new possibilities for a theatre company. If it's not possible to visit all the sites that are being toured to, it's essential that the dimensions and technical information about the sites are known as far in advance as possible. If the touring production is forced to adapt to a site, for example performing in a flat field one day followed by using a raised stage the next day, the show will need to have a technical rehearsal. This

Full House Theatre Company's production of Robin Hood, *part of its Welsh borderlands castles tour. (Photo: Keith Orton)*

enables the company to plot the lights and staging and helps the actors and stage management to familiarize themselves with the new surroundings.

Companies will generally try to rehearse the show a day before and at the same time as the show is to take place. This helps to recreate the conditions as accurately as possible. If a lighting and/or sound rig is being toured, it's useful to find a site that allows access to set up the day before the show is due to perform.

It's also important to find out if the site can be limited from public access during technical run-throughs and rehearsals. This can mean a quicker get in at each venue ultimately allowing more time for the fine-tuning of the technical equipment and rehearsals.

GETTING PERMISSION FOR THE SPACE

Companies first need to check with the council's community events officer. He/she will inform you about whether permission can be granted for use of the site, the particular negotiations that need to be made to secure the site and whether the proposed event clashes with others already planned. Armed with this information, a company will be able to project a costing for the show and apply for funding, if appropriate.

FUNDING

Like many theatre companies, it's fairly unusual for a company specializing in outdoor theatre to be fully self-sufficient. Invariably they require some kind of funding to make the work possible. Artistic directors and administrative staff are always thinking up new ways to get projects off the ground and exploring every avenue in the pursuit of funding. Funding available to companies varies from region to region and can depend on the nature of the show. For example, educational shows aimed at children will have different funding possibilities from a show that involves members of the local community.

Deadlines

With the initial concept or idea in hand, a company can apply for funding by submitting a proposal to the relevant funding bodies. These bodies, both private and public, often have financial deadlines to adhere to. It's very important to be aware of these deadlines. If they are missed, the funds will be allocated elsewhere, and it may mean that you have to wait another year before the production can go ahead.

Sources of funding

You should be aware that the sources of funding for registered charities are much greater than for non-charitable companies. It may neither be desirable nor achievable to make your company a registered charity, but it's worth considering in order to maximize your funding potential.

All companies need to work out a fundraising strategy, which begins by pinpointing the sources of funding. In the UK, initial funding is available in the following ways:

* *The Arts Council:* it gives funding directly to companies and theatres that match its current agenda.
* *Grants from the National Lottery:* The Arts and Heritage Lottery Fund has specific programmes that target areas it wants to encourage. A company may also apply for funding from other areas of the Lottery including health, welfare and education.
* *Local Authorities:* some authorities give funding in the form of revenue grants through their culture and leisure departments and often give support for specific projects. The local arts development officer and education officer can also help companies find out about other funding bodies or private trusts that may prove useful.
* *Grants from central government:* there are various government initiatives for deprived areas or areas of high unemployment. Companies that offer life skills to the local community or encourage community cohesion may be awarded funding for their projects.
* *Sponsorship by companies:* it's possible to receive sponsorship from a business directly or to receive sponsorship through the organization, Arts and Business. You may have to negotiate a sponsorship that requires, in return, publicity and public relations opportunities for the business such as advertising and complimentary tickets.
* *Grants from companies:* this would involve companies that have a particular interest in the themes of the show, the theatre company itself or an interest in the local area.
* *Grants from trusts, foundations and other charities:* funding is available for specific

projects from some registered charities, particularly if the themes of the piece of theatre reflect their ideology or the event presents a good publicity opportunity. There are grants available from various companies, depending on the area of the UK in which the show will take place. Companies such as the RC Sherriff Trust, which aims to develop the arts in the borough of Elmbridge in Surrey, and the Foundation for Sport and the Arts are just two such examples.

* *Individual donations:* interested individuals may fund, or help to fund, a production.
* *Community fundraising:* raising funds from raffles, events, collection boxes, sponsored walks etc.

The fundraising strategy should make sure that the relevant funding bodies know the companies' work and approve of their aims. The company should always keep a record of when money was applied for and to whom. There should also be a timetable in place for repeated applications (and at specific intervals) should the first application be unsuccessful.

Partnership and match funding

Most companies rely on funding from a mixture of the sources mentioned above and from 'partnership funding' or 'match funding'. Partnership funding works in a flowing way – a company has to demonstrate that it already has a certain amount of funding from another source before a second funding will be honoured. In match funding, a theatre company will have the money it has already raised 'matched' by the funding body to which it has applied.

Finding out more

There are several books and websites to help you find the funding options available and the best ways to apply. The charity Directory of Social Change produces an excellent starter guide called Effective Fundraising and also offers courses, which can be found at

The merchandise stall at Claremont, with stewards and security watching the performance.

A launch is a good time to organize publicity, gain permission to put up posters, ask local shop keepers to put flyers in their shops advertising the performance, and generally to spread awareness through the most useful form of advertising ... word of mouth.

www.dsc.org.uk. A wide range of information on funding options can also be found at www.fundraising.co.uk.

Launching your production

Other forms of revenue may include ticket sales and the sale of food and drink at the site. But in order to maximize profits from these sales, you will need effective publicity to inform your potential audience about the event. It is a great idea to launch the production through a social event. This allows you to invite potential sponsors and local council staff and, hopefully, create more funding. Having local press involved in the launch can also be an effective way of receiving free publicity. You might even turn the event into a fundraising opportunity that also raises money for the production.

NEGOTIATIONS AND LICENSING

There are some legal requirements to be fulfilled before a project can go ahead. A Licence for Public Performance application must be prepared and submitted to the local council. The Public Entertainment Licensing Act recently combined the licence for the sale of alcohol and the licence for the use of the space into one application process. This means that any licence to perform will automatically allow for the sale of alcohol. The production may need a Public Entertainment Licence, which is required for most events that have music, dancing or singing as a major part of the programme. Generally this depends on the length of a performance and the number of performers involved.

Applications to local councils

Applications for a production must be received at least fifty-six days before the performance date and will then be considered by the council's licensing committee. Only in exceptional circumstances will the Licensing Committee consider an application at shorter notice. In high periods of activity such as summer or Christmas, the waiting period may be longer. The council's licensing officer will be able to advise on this.

Licensing the space

Many local authorities have already identified areas of open space in their borough and issued them with a premises licence. These areas are ready for events to be held without the need for special application. However, companies will still need to apply to the council for use of this space, but the whole process shouldn't take as long and has a better chance of a favourable outcome than areas without a premises licence.

A theatre company wishing to hold an event on a specific piece of land needs first to seek the owner's permission. In general, at least three months notice is required for small to medium-sized events and up to six months for larger events. When permission has been granted, the company will then need to apply to the local council for a Temporary Event Notice.

Temporary Event Notice

Temporary Event Notices differ slightly depending on the local authority so make sure that you contact the council and ask for the specific rules that regulate licensable activities. Generally, there are various conditions involved in granting a Temporary Event Notice, and the local council judges each application on its merit. Only private events on your own premises, with no view to profit and no sale of alcohol, are exempt. If there is any doubt as to whether an event is licensable, contact the licensing department of the local council.

A company will need to submit two applications – one copy to the licensing authority and one to the local chief of police, who also has the power to object to the application on grounds of crime prevention.

Conditions

The performance of a play falls into the category of 'Regulated Entertainment' and comes with a list of conditions before permission is granted. Some of these conditions include: public liability insurance; that no more than twelve notices have been granted to the site in the previous twelve months; that first aid cover has been arranged; and that the total capacity – including actors, production staff and audience – does not exceed 499 people.

The time scale

It's worth noting that each Temporary Event Notice has a maximum duration of 96 hours (four days) and that the maximum aggregate duration at any individual premise is fifteen days in a calendar year. The decision on an application for a Temporary Event Notice will typically take about ten working days, although this can vary from council to council and most would wish to receive the application at least one calendar month before the date of the event. This will enable the licensing body and the police to examine the application and may help to resolve any issues or possible objections.

6 WEATHER, SEASON AND TIME

It is well known that the English love to talk about the weather, and what better opportunity than when faced with the prospect of staging or watching a theatre show outdoors. As a nation, we seem to take an almost macabre joy in never quite knowing what might befall us. Having watched and worked on countless outdoor theatre productions over the years, I have witnessed just about every type of weather imaginable.

Both outdoor theatre audiences and performers are surprisingly resilient to most weather conditions. However, precautions should always be taken when embarking on an outdoor run as the weather can be alarmingly unpredictable. Very few theatre companies dare brave the outdoors during winter, preferring to stick to the potentially warmer and drier summer months. There is also the question of venue availability as many of the outdoor venues used by theatre companies only open in the summer months. But even performing during the summer by no means guarantees a dry or warm performance so outdoor theatre companies should have strategies in place to cope with (almost) every eventuality.

AUDIENCE GOOD WILL

There is an unspoken camaraderie between the audience and performers when weather does disrupt the show, and it can often be one of the most thrilling moments. No performer can ignore the rustling of raincoats or the sudden opening of umbrellas. It is a moment for the performer to share a joke with the audience or ad lib about the conditions – or, if brave enough, even steal an audience member's umbrella. It is partly for the unknown eventualities that many people go to an outdoor theatre production, and the wet weather or high winds do not have to spoil the occasion.

DESIGN

Designing for an outdoor theatre show entails a different approach from an indoor theatre. There are a variety of different factors to consider: the lack of light, though not usually from the beginning of the piece; the changes and effects of the weather and the challenge of using sound.

The set and costumes should help the actor to hold the audience's attention and must work effectively in wind, rain, sun and even snow.

Essentially, the design elements should be bold and confident in establishing what they are trying to communicate. Subtle detail and ambiguity will invariably be lost outdoors. Whatever the conditions, it should still be possible to focus audience members by creating bold design elements that inform them of the

'And the weather for me after so many years of doing this becomes anthropomorphic. I sometimes sit for half an hour or so watching the sky as a storm approaches, asking it not to come. But of course it is indifferent. It will come if it will come – and it puts us in our place and what we do in its place. There is no opportunity to be self-important working outdoors.'

(Pete Talbot,
The Rude Mechanical Theatre Company)

settings and characters. The fabrics and set pieces in a performance outdoors should always be durable enough to withstand the elements. There are certain materials that work better than others while techniques used for indoor theatre may prove completely unsuitable in outdoor conditions.

Wearing shoes suitable to the surface

From a costume perspective, if it's possible design each outfit with shoes that have a good grip, especially if the playing area is grass. Plimsolls are ideal as they have a good grip sole, and most performers are used to wearing them. If the production requires shoes that are unsuitable for the surface, make sure the performers have had plenty of rehearsal time to get used to them – and on the surface they'll actually be performing on.

'We regard it like a sporting event – if it rains we try and continue until it becomes too distracting. Slight rain tends to focus the audience.'

(Jonathan Petherbridge, artistic director,
London Bubble Theatre Company)

WEATHER

Cancellations

Most outdoor theatre companies have a non-cancellation policy and reserve the right to stop and start the show as the weather or other disruptions dictate. If conditions do become untenable, making it virtually impossible to hear the actors, the stage manager may take the decision to stop the performance until conditions improve. This will inevitably prompt the audience and actors alike to run for the nearest available cover, which will most likely be the interval bar. If there are any musicians in the play, they may also take this opportunity to have an impromptu musical session.

If a performance cannot commence or is stopped because of the weather, it is established practice to offer the audience seats for another performance, but not to refund the tickets. Naturally, this is at the discretion of each company. However, most companies will push through to the end of a performance, even with a dwindling number of audience members, for this very reason.

It can be very costly to offer an entire audience free tickets for another night, and if a show is already popular, there are the problems of availability – and whether an audience member can actually attend another show. It is a situation that is best avoided, and no one can be blamed for the weather conditions. So it may seem somewhat absurd at the time, but struggling through to the end of the performance is usually the best practice. A theatre company that largely relies on ticket sales to pay for the production is already taking a risk by performing outside. This is because many audience members wait until the day of the performance to purchase tickets, and if particularly unpleasant weather is forecast, ticket sales will inevitably drop, with the financial implications that that involves.

A cancelled performance of **The Bridge** *by Mimbre as part of the National Theatre's 'watch this space' outdoor events programme, 2007. Because of the rain, the stage was deemed too dangerous and slippery for this acrobatic performance. The National Theatre supplied mats and rain outfits for the audience.*

'I do sometimes wish for the physical comfort of indoor theatre. I have worked indoors occasionally, but the naked intensity of working outdoors, especially with an audience who doesn't usually go to the theatre or who isn't used to our style then seeing it gradually warm to us, is very special. Then there are the chance contributions of nature or of other people's worlds: a bell ringing at the right time, the moon rising, moths in the gaslight. It is special – partly because it is a partnership with chance.'

(Pete Talbot,
The Rude Mechanical Theatre Company)

This tablecloth in The Princess, the Palace and the Ice Cold Bath *needed a string of lead weight sewn into the hem to keep it in place whilst the banquet was brought out.*
(Photo: Kim Stapff)

Wind

Wind is such an unknown quantity in outdoor theatre and can be a blessing for some productions and a real hindrance for others. The right strength of wind can make flags fly and ships' sails balloon, but it can also carry an actor's voice away and, in severe cases, even some of the props and set. The key is to be prepared for the eventuality of wind, especially if the site(s) are situated in exposed areas such as coastal locations or open fields. It is important to take into account which part of the country the show will take place in. There are parts of the UK, especially towards Scotland, that are well known to experience high winds.

Preparation of the design
Whatever the location of the site, it's crucial to design the set, costumes and props with windy conditions in mind. The presence of high winds shouldn't render any design elements dangerous or unusable. It is equally important not to rely on the wind to make any of the design elements work. There is a fine balance to be struck here so examine the locations carefully – bearing in mind the time of year, as June, for example, can offer quite different weather conditions from September – and assess an average wind 'norm'. The design can then be created to some degree around this prediction.

ABOVE: **Rain-drenched production** *of* **Merlin's Child** *at the* **Minack Theatre** *in* **2006.**

RIGHT: *Incorporating* **umbrellas** *into a costume design in* **Mirage** *at Greenwich Docklands International Festival, 2007.* (Photo: Doug Southall, Pepper Pictures)

A production that needs to harness the wind, perhaps to help create a scene or give the costumes movement, can employ the use of a wind machine on calm days to achieve a comparable effect. Similarly, if a company needs to control the wind, it can build windshields into the set design to protect the space in adverse conditions. However, using a wind machine or a windshield will have an impact on the budget of the show: the get in and out times will lengthen, more transport may be needed and there may be increased build costs of the set. Therefore, if the show is designed to work regardless of whether there is or isn't wind, it will ultimately save time and money.

Fabrics needed for the production – and not intended as flags – should be weighted or battened down so they stay in place. This applies to anything from a tablecloth on set to the banner advertising the production at the site entrance.

Rain

Rain is possibly the least welcome weather condition for companies staging a show outside. Rain is invariably the main cause for terminating, or severely delaying, a production. It can cause flooding and surfaces to become slippery, which can in turn endanger actors and audience alike. Obviously, it can also have an adverse affect on electrical equipment. However, some of these problems can quite easily be avoided. If a suitable location is found in the first place and strategies put in place to deal with the rain, there is a much greater chance of avoiding cancellations and delays.

The problem of mud

If the location has turf or earth flooring, the onset of rain can easily turn the space into a mud bath. Not only will the audience be continually traversing the same space, the actors will be carrying out the same movements again and again. If mud is a problem, it's a

'And of course you get wet. Very wet. You explore aspects of wetness that can only be appreciated when all your costumes (you'll probably have at least three, because it's unlikely you'll enjoy the luxury of playing only one part) are so wet that getting into them in time for arriving for your cue is a frantic backstage wrestling match.'

(Martin Thomas, actor, Illyria Company)

good idea to move the audience's entrances and exits and shift the playing area (if possible). If this isn't an option, then the laying of straw or sawdust can help to dry the ground, provided the venue's owners have no objection, and the placement of rush mats may save both the actors and audience from increasingly muddy clothes.

Drying off

If the venue has an onsite wardrobe department, it's a good idea to find out whether they have access to tumble dryers in the eventuality of a downpour, especially if shows are closely packed or touring back to back. If the show is touring to venues without maintenance staff, then a strategy should be put in place to allow for trips to a launderette to dry off costumes between shows. It's neither good for an actor's health to put on wet costumes nor for the costumes, which will deteriorate over time.

Designing costumes for extreme weather

There are some simple costume techniques to make the performers' time on stage more bearable. For example, it's a very nice touch to design a raincoat in the same style as the actor's costume. It may not be needed, but can be worn if rain does arrive or looks like it might. Similarly, an umbrella or a parasol can be added to complement a character's costume and can perform the dual task of protecting the actor from the sun and the rain.

The use of such practical props also opens up the possibility of either lending it to an audience member when not needed or borrowing a 'prop' from someone when it is. It's a very common convention in outdoor theatre and can only further engage the audience. When designing costumes for outdoor theatre, try to remember that the fabric will inevitably take a battering. If it's not the rain, it might be the sun so choose fabrics that will last in adverse conditions. It's also advisable not to design a particularly precious or expensive outfit. Even if it's protected by an umbrella or raincoat, the effect of being outdoors will eventually seep through and ruin anything not sturdy enough.

The use of umbrellas
Some outdoor theatres will allow the audience to use umbrellas in the event of rain, but will invariably ask for co-operation in keeping them held low so the people behind can see the

'After that rain-drenched show, I created cloaks for the actors in case another storm hit and always had extra cloaks for the warriors because it was extremely important for them to stay warm as they were lying on the floor pretending to be dead for a good few minutes at the end of the show.'

(Emma Louise Morton, designer, *Merlin's Child*, Minack Theatre, 2006)

performance. Some companies won't allow the use of umbrellas. This may seem unfair, but it's because of the layout of the stage in relation to the audience area. They have to take into account whether the seating is fixed and how closely packed the audience is. Umbrellas are fine if the sightlines are good and the audience has room to manoeuvre. But if the space is tight or the seating fixed, umbrellas can cause more problems than they solve, agitating audience members and performers alike.

Umbrellas are perfectly acceptable for use by an audience in inclement weather conditions where sightlines and space are not an issue. National Theatre, 2006.

Using water to your advantage

Because outdoor theatre has to be prepared for the onset of rain, some companies actively use water in their performance as an opportunity to use water safely in a theatrical context. A touring show called Bollywood Steps by Nutkhut Theatre Company included a large water effect that shot thirty feet of water into the air purposely to create the wet sari scene. Avanti Display, the company responsible for this effect, had just produced an adaptation of Shakespeare's *The Tempest* on London's Southbank, which also used huge water jets to recreate the storm in the play. *The Sultan's* *Elephant*, an outdoor theatre piece by French company Royale Deluxe, includes an enormous, forty-two ton elephant that occasionally treats the crowd to huge bursts of water from its trunk. So if the space allows it, sometimes being wet can be used to the piece's advantage.

Advantages of being outdoors

Many theatre practitioners take advantage of the possibilities that outdoor theatre provides, most of which are simply impossible indoors. As well as being able to use water more safely, fire can also be employed outdoors with

The Sultan's Elephant, *created by French company Royale Deluxe, in which the elephant squirts water from its trunk at intervals along the route, seen here in London, 2006.* (Photo: Keith Orton)

pyrotechnics, fireworks and naked flames. Naked flames, including burning torches, candles and bonfires, can work spectacularly once the sun has set. However, any production should be wary of relying on them for illumination as they not only give a weak and undirected light, but the arrival of rain can quickly make the light redundant. If a performer needs to rely on a naked flame, for example a match or candle, and the weather conditions aren't suitable, it's wise to have as standby a battery-operated alternative.

The sun

Most outdoor theatre companies always hope for an abundance of sun during their performance, as it seems to be the magic ingredient for drawing crowds. Also, sunny conditions mean that the actors will remain dry during the performance and that the production team doesn't need to worry about the electrics or cancelling the show.

However, the sun can cause problems for the cast, either through sunburn or heat exhaustion. Should rehearsals or technical run-throughs take place outside during the day, it's important to ensure that everyone is covered up and reminded to apply sun cream and wear a hat. If rehearsals or run-throughs are away from any shops or amenities, it is advisable to provide plenty of water. I have worked on a few shows that have disregarded some of these rules – more by accident than design – and both cast and crew have suffered from dehydration.

A well-prepared cast member avoiding the direct sun during an all-day rehearsal on site, **The Princess, the Palace and the Ice Cold Bath**, *2006*. *(Photo: Kim Stapff)*

The audience

The company should make sure the audience is comfortable if temperatures are unusually high. This is especially relevant for a matinée, as these often play to a younger audience. A company would be wise to have some hats and sunscreen on standby to give to people who've failed to bring any. Hats don't have to be expensive: they can be quickly fashioned from newspaper or another material in keeping with the design of the show.

The stage

The positioning of the stage in relation to the sun is an important factor. It's stating the obvious, but it's not advisable to position the stage with the sun shining directly into the eyes of the audience. Equally, it's not a good idea to have the sun shining directly into the eyes of the performers (especially if the performers are working on a raised platform). This is another good reason for visiting the proposed site during the time of the performance, both during the day and at night. An ideal position is to have some shade for the stage or for the stage to be at an angle to the sun's path.

The musicians

If the production uses musicians – or an orchestra – and they are placed off stage, they will need to be housed in a gazebo or cover of some kind in order to keep them and their instruments protected from the weather. If the musicians have been provided with costumes, these could be in keeping with the general costume design so that they become part of the show. This is particularly appropriate if they are to be clearly seen by the audience. It is also worthwhile that the musicians have a change of costume in case of rain.

THE SEASONS

Several companies are reviving traditional and pagan festivals in Britain and creating outdoor theatre based on ancient rites. As people become more concerned about the environment, there is greater interest in the land and

> 'The late-twentieth century is struggling to sustain a sense of the natural world within its urban enclaves. The reintroduction of celebrations of the seasons on the urban streets where they were enjoyed before, when the seasons still affected urban life, is a way to reconnect with nature and its vital product, food.'
>
> (Sonia Ritter, artistic director, the Lions part Theatre Company)

Musicians in a gazebo, at the edge of the stage, keeping themselves and their instruments safe from the weather, Merlin's Child, Minack Theatre, 2006. (Photo: Keith Orton)

Musicians appropriately clothed for the production of **The Persians** *by Thiasos Theatre Company, Oxford, 2006.*

how society engages with it. A whole host of festivals celebrating the seasons and old farming practices has re-emerged, and there are numerous stories and characters to be rediscovered in these ancient practices. One of the foremost theatre companies performing work based on the seasons is the Lions part.

The Lions part Theatre Company

The Lions part's ever increasing repertoire of outdoor shows include many that are based on texts from the fifteenth century, such as *May Games, Olde Summer's Wakes and Revels, The Spring's Glorie, October Plenty* and *Twelfth Night. October Plenty* and *Twelfth Night* are performed on the Thames Bankside,

Southwark, each year and celebrate the seasons with games, old customs, music, dance and the appearance of the 'Green Man' in various guises. *Twelfth Night*, performed after Christmas, is an ancient mummers' play that the Lions part has since revived. *October Plenty* is an autumn harvest celebration that renews many old traditions, including the execution of John Barleycorn and the Corn Queene.

Choosing a season

Companies that explore the possibilities of celebrating seasons other than summer will often be richly rewarded with larger audiences. This is simply because of the lack of competition from other venues outside of the summer

93

An incredibly wet Twelfth Night performed after Christmas by the brave Lion's Part Theatre Company on London's Bankside, Southwark, 2007.

An audience with an indomitable spirit watching the Lion's Part perform in January 2007.

months. There aren't necessarily any special considerations when performing seasonal productions, apart from the drop in temperature and the shorter days that the winter and autumn seasons bring. But with appropriate planning and design, any outdoor production can still work in these conditions.

TIME CONSIDERATIONS

The time of a performance will depend on all manner of conditions, such as the season it's being performed in, the amount of natural light the company needs to work with and the audience it's aimed at. Evening performances can realistically begin at any time between six

'Welfare State International always placed its celebrations at seasonal crossovers. In the 1970s it performed mumming plays at Christmas, and other pageants at various seasonal points. It was very aware of the farming calendars, which were overlaid by pagan, Celtic and the church calendar rituals, claiming that people still derive pleasure from being reminded of the roots of our past.'

(John Fox, in his book *Eyes on Stalks*)

and eight o'clock. Earlier shows tend to draw a younger audience, and the production is more likely to play to children, especially if there are matinées as well. If a production starts later than eight o'clock, it may be that the show relies on darkness in order to achieve certain effects with lighting or staging.

Lighting and effects

Lighting will obviously have to be considered if the performance's running time goes beyond dusk. This creates a variety of possibilities and challenges of how the space should be lit. The solution may well be more a matter of budget than aesthetics, but generally most shows use some sort of electrical lighting to illuminate the space. This is something to consider very early on in the design.

The first half of the production, and even some of the second, may not require any illumination. But some sort of lighting is almost inevitable at some stage. Like any production

A performer interacting with the audience during Five Get Famous *by The Rude Mechanical Theatre Company, 2007.*

indoors, this throws up a range of challenges. Factors that work in natural light may become a hindrance when artificial light is used, and conversely new opportunities may open up when lighting is introduced. If the production requires the use of fireworks or pyrotechnics, as impressive as they are, they can be expensive and are sometimes lost unless seen against a dark sky. They should therefore only be used when they will be seen to best effect.

Audiences

Audiences of daytime and evening performances are clearly visible to a performer, unlike in indoor theatre. The performer cannot ignore the presence of an audience and ideally shouldn't try to. The audience is an integral element of any outdoor show – much more than in an indoor venue – as, invariably, it inhabits the same space as the performance. Any production should, at the very least, acknowledge this unique relationship, and the best productions actively use it to their advantage.

Running time

The actual running time of a production shouldn't exceed two and a half hours including an interval, or ninety minutes without an interval. This isn't a strict rule, but an audience's attention will inevitably waver, and all the hard work up until now will be lost if the production goes on for too long. One complaint that audiences make time and time again about outdoor performances is that they are too long with too much dialogue.

Shaping the piece
Many directors find it difficult to edit a script or delete scenes that they favour. Some directors pride themselves on changing nothing in a script and remaining true to the author's intention. This is commendable, and is more achievable in a seated, air-conditioned indoor theatre. But slavish devotion to a piece ignores the very real constraints of outdoor theatre and such a practice in modern outdoor theatre remains doubtful. With the inevitability of an audience being distracted by outside interference, or simply missing some of the dialogue, there seems little point in any production devotedly following a text that was never intended to be performed outdoors. A good rule to follow is to be less precious about the piece and think more about the welfare of the audience.

7 DESIGN TECHNIQUES

The design for a piece of outdoor theatre uses many of the skills of an indoor performance, although there are techniques (mentioned throughout the book) that are often employed specifically for outdoor work. The fundamental job of a designer is to aid the audience's understanding of the piece in accordance with the director's vision. The most pressing points to bear in mind are:

* The size of the space
* The get in and get out implications
* The weather restrictions (and possibilities)
* The budget
* The audience.

TELLING THE STORY

In indoor theatre, the text can often work alone to tell the story. Unfortunately, in outdoor theatre spoken dialogue alone cannot be depended on to deliver the narrative. This makes the designer's job more difficult as the audience may also need to refer to the design to understand the story. The set, costume, lighting or sound, or the collaboration of these elements, needs to tell the story coherently, and, consequently, has to work much harder in an outdoor setting. However, the designer is rarely alone in taking decisions. In most cases, the director and possibly the performers will be involved in all of the design elements and consulted on a regular basis during the production process. Their involvement is even more

'Traditional theatre employs a set designer to design the pre-ordained space at the start, according to instructions from both playwright and director, and allows actors limited time to inhabit the designer's created world.'

(Jon Oram, Claque Theatre Company)

important if the show is devised, site specific or uses techniques from physical theatre.

ENCOURAGING THE CREATIVE PROCESS

During the early stages of production, it's a good idea to spend time in rehearsals and get to know the performers well. It can be incredibly advantageous to find out how they move and what their specific skills are. Even before the piece has been blocked, it's also useful to take along an assortment of props and a dressing-up box full of hats, wigs and coats for the performers to play with in rehearsals. Not only does this help to inspire their creativity, but also makes the performers – and director – more aware of the possibilities that costumes and props can bring. Having tangible items in rehearsal will often lead to the creation of a scene, or elements within a scene, based on the use of props and costume.

Having a collection of items in rehearsal also teaches performers to think of costume in

Performers in Taste, *produced by Chipping Norton Theatre, utilizing many of the props to create the scene. Normandy, France 2005.*

a more integral way, rather than as something they put on at the last minute. The same principle applies to any props used in rehearsal or during the devising process. Basic items such as cloths, brooms, boxes, kitchen utensils and pieces of wood are immensely useful for performers to have access to and can also lead to other design ideas when moved around, turned upside down or manipulated as part of a scene.

CHOOSING THE SITE

It's important for a designer to be involved in

the production process right from the very beginning and, ideally, help to decide on the site itself. In general, it's always better to choose a space that can be intimate in order to allow an audience to become as immersed in the 'world' of the play as possible. The type of outdoor theatre, of course, will largely determine this, but a design will usually be more effective if it is focused and capable of fully inhabiting the space. A designer should always bear in mind the timescale and budget restrictions. These may simply not allow bigger areas to be dressed as effectively as a contained area would be.

EXPLOITING THE SPACE

It is always a good idea for designers to consider the show as a complete experience, rather than merely thinking about the action on stage. By the very nature of the space, outdoor theatre is much more of a holistic event. From the minute people arrive – from the ritual of unpacking picnics and even a trip to the lavatory – a designer can exploit their experiences and immerse them in the space.

There are numerous techniques that can be used: playing music (either live or recorded), having the characters greet the audience, putting up sculptures, pieces of costume or set along the path leading to the performance space. These techniques will both intrigue an audience and help them to make immediate connections with the piece. The experiences do not have to be extravagant, expensive or shocking – although being greeted by an enormous stilt-walking spider at a performance of Claremont's *Fête Champêtre* certainly made an impact!

MAKING A START

It's always difficult to know where to start implementing ideas as a designer may well be waiting on other elements of the production, especially if the piece is devised. But if possible, decide on the definite ideas early on and negotiate a 'to do list' with the director regarding the most important items needed in rehearsal. This will help both you and the performers immensely. Trying out the different elements as early as possible will pinpoint any potential problems, and you will inevitably have to make changes to the design. It's always better to know these problems early on as time is invariably short and presenting a crucial design element that doesn't work can be disastrous.

It's also wise to keep the director involved during the making stages, rather than pre-

Performer with a cut-out sheep, exploring the use of the car park as an extension of the performance area. Caer Llan Research Project. (Photo: Keith Orton)

senting him or her with the finished article. Ask him/her to view design pieces in the various stages of production, as this will prevent problems of communication between you both. Try to get items to a limited stage of practicality, without necessarily finishing them completely, so they can be introduced into rehearsal (and into the outdoor arena). It can be a huge waste of time and effort, not to mention extremely frustrating, to finish a piece only to discover it doesn't work as intended and needs to be adapted or worse still, cut altogether.

Unfinished cart being tried out in rehearsals to make sure that it fulfils all its functions before being painted and finished entirely. (Photo: Kim Stapff)

FINALIZING DESIGNS

A general design rule is to set a date with the director when all the designs should be finalized. Some directors get carried away by the increasing possibilities presented by an outdoor environment and the design list can become never-ending. So always choose a date that you both agree on, which will be the very final sign-off of designs. If the director does come up with new ideas after that date, you are in a much better position to decline or at least limit their execution. It is always better to cap the amount of set, prop and costume elements required to what is reasonably attainable in the time and budget. Saying yes to every new idea will simply mean the depletion of resources and, ultimately, will lead to poor quality of the work.

SET AND PROPS

A set isn't normally the focus in an outdoor venue, as the location should be doing a lot of the work in supporting the theme(s) of the production. The main reason for set pieces will normally be to fulfil a particular practical function, such as raising the actors above the audience (and presenting possibilities for quick entrances or exits through the use of trap-doors), to mask an area or to allow for an off-stage. Because of the nature of outdoor theatre, props, rather than set changes, are more likely to be used to denote a scene change as nothing can be flown or trucked in from the wings.

PREPARING THE DESIGN

Outdoor theatre sets are usually designed with model pieces rather than a complete model box. These pieces are easily manipulated and a useful tool for the director and designer to play with. A ground plan with marked entrances and exits should be drawn up and is invaluable for working out scene transitions. It is always a good idea to look at what is indispensable to the set rather than what is desirable. For example, if a set fundamentally requires a rope across the stage and a sheet to be hung from it, then start with this idea as your template. You can then begin to think about other elements that will enhance the audience's understanding. Is there writing on the sheet, how is it attached, what colour is it, is it pinned to the ground, do the performers interact with it? So start with what is needed and then bring in more elements to support the creative vision.

These set elements should be chosen to signify the scene or setting with as little effort as possible in order to concentrate design interpretation energies and enable fluid scene changes. In the same way that a costume should clearly and quickly identify a character, the piece of set or prop should do the same with the scene. This is why the use of symbols and icons is so prevalent in outdoor theatre. The set elements can of course interact with the performers to give them greater significance. In this way, the designer, director and performers will discover which scenic elements and props are integral to the production. It also means there is less to build, transport and set up.

Miniature house carried in a hod to signify the sudden building of new houses in the area. **Seven Streams** *community play, designed by Nicola Fitchett, Tonbridge, 2007. (Photo: Nicola Fitchett)*

Making the set last
In an indoor theatre, there is little possibility of an audience coming into contact with the set, so it only needs to be rigorous enough to cope with the demands of being onstage. But an outdoor set is much more likely to come into contact with an audience and it's certainly worth planning for this. Your set may also need to be better built in order to survive the various challenges of the weather. Whether the production runs for one night or over several months, the set still has to look good and function properly.

The overall design process
As a general rule, the design process of outdoor theatre is more organic than indoor theatre. It primarily involves using the site as a catalyst for ideas, together with themes brought about from rehearsal. In an indoor theatre space, a designer might be more concerned with just the set and its creative impact within the playing area. The space between the stage and the audience is already defined so it's an element that does not have to be considered.

For a designer, an outdoor theatre space presents a wider range of possibilities for audience and staging configurations. By working closely with the director and other members of the production, a solution will be agreed upon regarding the overall design. If staging is required (and it may not be) it is then the

'As well as the primary interactions involving audience and performers there are the interactions between the different production elements – scenery, costumes, props, lighting, sound and so on. Technicians should have input in every phase of the "making", workshop and rehearsals. Technicians should participate all the way through and during performances be as free to improvise as the performers. Let's ban light boards locked into presets, only then can the possibility exist for "performing technicians".'

(Jon Oram, director, Claque Theatre Company)

'decoration' of the space that needs to be considered. This staging will need to be made from materials with the correct weight, texture, feel, colour and density, to express the play.

It's always a good idea not to be too dogmatic when approaching the stage setting. Leave room for flexibility and the possibilities of scenic improvisation. Try to design a strong theme to express the play from beginning to end and communicate this to the director and performers. Then concentrate on getting your design theme into rehearsal as early as possible.

Using only what's necessary

You should only use or make what's really needed. This keeps a production focused on the absolute essential elements, rather than encumbering the space with lots of unnecessary props or set pieces. Allow the performers to use set pieces and props in imaginative ways and to use them again in another way if possible. Any prop or set almost needs to 'earn' the right to be on stage by fulfilling as many functions as possible or by being absolutely crucial to the story. The lengthy trawling of set pieces on and off the stage to establish a time or place can be tedious for the audience. There are invariably quicker and more ingenious ways to inform an audience. If a theatrical convention or practice is employed in a show, it must be done throughout to enable the audience to recognize it. Once a theatrical convention has been established, every piece of costume and set must be examined closely to make sure that it fulfils the established convention's criteria. This can then become an easy and direct way of informing the audience as to what is happening without the use of huge scene or costume changes.

Looking up

A designer should always remember the space available above head height where props and set elements can also be used. This becomes especially relevant if the audience is at the same level as the performers or where the performers move among the audience and sightlines could become an issue. There is then the potential of action being missed by the audience. The use of flags, banners or even sets carried on poles or worn as headgear can signify a scene change or act as backdrop.

Lighting

To see how a design element might look under lights, a designer will often examine samples of paint and fabrics in the dark, using a torch for illumination. Alternatively, he/she may use a model box with miniature lights with the appropriate gels in place. These techniques are only relevant if the production or part of the production takes place during darkness. It's also worth noting that it's rare to have complete darkness, with abundant street lighting or even the moon to help light the area. Many outdoor shows begin in daylight and finish in near darkness so it is important that the design works well in both situations.

Boats made from withy and muslin attached to hard hats. International Festival of the Sea, Portsmouth, 2001.

Making an impact

It may be the case that the playing area itself, or an element within the playing area, has to make a specific impact. A director will often have crucial moments that he/she believes the story hinges on, and it's the job of the designer to make sure those moments are realized as powerfully as possible. The designer can then see what further possibilities there are or the adjustments that are necessary to accommodate other elements.

A set within a set

Anyone designing for outdoors has to accept the premise of a 'set within a set'. This means the set on stage has to work within the space surrounding it. There is little to be gained from building a wall around your set to 'enclose' it, effectively trying to recreate an indoor theatre space. Designers working in an indoor theatre will be accustomed to working within certain conventions, i.e. the 'black box' space of the playing area. They will also enjoy other design opportunities, such as using gauze, painted scenery, lighting specific areas of the stage and so on. Designers of an outdoor space need to understand that their backdrop is the set. The space around the playing area cannot and should not be ignored. All they can do is design scenic pieces that will work with or against what exists around it.

USING THE ENVIRONMENT

An interesting approach to the solution of design is to use what is already natural in the space and gently manipulate it into an appropriate playing area. For example, some productions have created raised playing areas from sand or mud, while others have made sculptures inspired by the surrounding flora and fauna. Without the introduction of any man-made elements, this technique immediately transforms the space into a stage, especially when performers interact with it.

103

Scoop's production of **Helen of Troy** *at the venue More London. The stage of this new amphitheatre built next to Tower Bridge offers an office interior backdrop that is difficult to ignore.*

What makes this choice of design more exciting is the ambiguity for the audience. It allows the designer to play with the concept of seen/unseen, real/unreal, made/unmade, whilst an audience cannot tell what has naturally occurred in the space and what new elements have been introduced. By simply manipulating the natural environment of the space, the site can surprise and delight an audience in many more ways than a conventional set.

Making a mark

Although this is a rare occurrence in outdoor theatre, some companies design a set or an element of the production that can be left permanently in the space. Obviously, to do this, the company should use either a biodegradable set or seek the permission of the site owners to leave it there. It's an interesting idea to leave a permanent or semi-permanent mark on the landscape as theatre, by its very nature, is transient and ephemeral.

COSTUME

Whatever the design for the costumes, always bear in mind that they have to be durable, wearable and 'seeable' (if an audience can't quickly identify the costume, it's not working).

It's only when designers ignore the realities of the outdoors and the space the performers are working in that costumes fail to work effectively. If the production needs costumes off the peg, then try to find fabrics that will work in outdoor conditions and don't slavishly follow a design principle. It simply won't work.

If the production requires costumes to be made from scratch, it's imperative to choose the right type of material. Quick-drying synthetic fabrics can be great for making costumes. They're produced in vibrant colours, which is useful as the sun can have a bleaching effect on colour. Modern synthetic fabrics are extremely lightweight and won't soak up water, unlike natural fibres. They're also cheap enough to be used abundantly and textured if necessary.

Choosing the right fabrics

A commonly used fabric in outdoor theatre is 'ripstop', a hybrid between plastic and fabric. Although not suitable for period pieces, it's great for physical performers. It has a lot of movement in windy conditions – many kites and windsurfs are made from ripstop because of its ability to hold air – is durable and can be cut without ripping or fraying. Ripstop is perfect for costumes or set pieces that need to harness the wind. Feathers and furry fabrics can go limp and look tired when exposed to too much moisture, either from the rain or an actor's perspiration in hot weather. Thick and

The audience is guided by simple wooden fences built from 'found' sticks at the site. (Photo: Keith Orton)

> 'When choosing fabrics for outdoor costumes it is useful to do a test to check how transparent the fabric might become in the rain. This can help avoid the embarrassment of partial nudity or revealing underwear that is out of period with the outer costume.'
>
> (Keith Orton, theatre designer)

heavy fabrics, such as velvet or brocade, may be suitable for period costumes but can make the performer unbearably hot in warm weather.

Also, most velvet and brocade are dry clean only, which can quickly become expensive. Even if it were possible to wash them, these thick and absorbent fabrics take a long time to dry, which means they're less practical for an outdoor run. If they get dirty on a regular basis, which is almost a certainty, they're also much harder to clean. Velvet, for example, is easily marked and the pile can be quickly flattened by water. Rain can cause some fabrics to shrink and if there are no drying facilities on

Performers in A Midsummer Night's Dream, *Creation Theatre Company, Oxford, 2005. It is especially important for physical performers and stilt wearers to wear comfortable, lightweight clothing in which they are able to move freely. Costumes designed by Kate Unwin. (Photo: Creation Theatre Company)*

site, the costumes may not be dry for the next performance. Not only is this uncomfortable for the performer, it could hinder their progress in a quick change. Finally, be aware that constant rain can fade fabrics and cause dyed material to run. So a washing test is essential, especially if two or more contrasting colours are going to be used in one outfit.

Merlin's Child

A good, if unfortunate, example of great design that fell foul of bad weather was a show called *Merlin's Child*, performed at the Minack Theatre in Cornwall. The production employed an array of real and fake fur in its design. Besides the moral dilemma posed by the wearing of animal skins, fur can also make a performer extremely hot and may start to smell when wet. Although the choice of costume was appropriate to the theme of the production, it couldn't have been more unsuitable for the particular week the production was playing. Unfortunately, the show experienced torrential downpours and consequently, the wardrobe team had the task of trying to get everything dry for each new show.

'The long-haired fake fur was completely soaked through and horrendous to dry, the only way to do it was with hairdryers. This was difficult as any more than two hairdryers and the electricity circuit would trip. Once the fake fur got wet it took a few days to dry. The only thing to hope for was a few hours of sunshine the next morning. With the costumes for this show being mainly leather and fur you can't just put them in the tumble dryer.

I also discovered that leather is not as sturdy and waterproof as I had anticipated, especially when it is old. The day after the storm I found that the leather armour pieces I had hired had become so hard that pieces started to snap off or tear. Leather boots had suddenly become two sizes too small and there was nowhere to go to hire or buy period boots. It took two people to squeeze them on the actor and he had to perform until they stretched back into shape.'

(Emma Louise Morton, designer of *Merlin's Child*, 2006)

Backstage at the Minack Theatre, designer Emma Louise Morton tries to dry out some of the costumes after a particularly torrential downpour. (Photo: Keith Orton)

Cast of **Merlin's Child** *at the Minack Theatre, 2006. The photograph shows the abundance of real and fake fur in the show and the use of body paint. (Photo: Keith Orton)*

Using the body

One of the main areas of costume routinely ignored is the actual body of a performer. Skin is in fact a great waterproof material and offers a surface that can be drawn or painted on, and dries instantly. Waterproof and smudge-proof body paint, available from specialized make-up suppliers, will adequately withstand a good deal of rain. The application of hairspray to 'fix' a tattoo once it has dried will further help to keep it from smudging. Body paint can also be mixed with talcum powder to give it a chalky finish.

If the performer needs a quick or less permanent solution for body art, tattooed skin effects can be achieved by using fabric paints or acrylic mixed with textile medium applied directly on to tights or a sheer stretch fabric such as 'powernet'. Powernet comes in a range of thickness and colour, so be sure to choose the most lightweight, flesh tone.

Learn to be bold

When thinking about the costumes for an outdoor production, try to incorporate bold symbolic elements and easily identifiable stereotypes. If the performers play more than one role, there's rarely time to establish each character with a big costume change. If the performers have a quick change and are essentially dressing the character with one or two elements, make sure the elements you choose are immediately recognizable for an audience. Try not to be too prescriptive with your choices as the final elements are often worked out through discussion or workshops with the performer and may be integral to their movements and characterization.

Clown items, such as body padding and false noses, are excellent devices for quick changes as they immediately alter the shape of the performer. Body padding can also be sewn into an item of clothing in order to make the change even quicker. Remember, it's not essential for actors to change entire outfits in order to change their character. Audiences often like nothing more than the simplicity of seeing a coat being worn inside out or the addition of a hat to signify a different character.

Body padding can be used dramatically to change body shapes and create larger than life characters. International Festival of the Sea, Portsmouth, 2006. Costumes designed by Julia Knight.
(Photo: Julia Knight)

Going beyond the costume

Outdoor theatrical performances often use devices that cross the boundary between puppetry and costume. There are numerous techniques a designer can use: stilts, arm extensions, distended body shapes (using padding), headdresses and masks. Before using these techniques, it's important for the designer first to explore their possibilities with the actors. This is because the performer may not be comfortable or able to cope with the extra demands of certain costumes. Masks, for example, completely change a person's spatial awareness. So ensure the performers have enough time to rehearse with the costumes and are comfortable using them. There may be a great deal of 'tweaking' involved with more physical costumes, so bear this in mind when designing intricate pieces.

Hiring

Fortunately, not everything will need to be made from scratch. For a relatively short run, costumes and props can easily be hired. The

Performer dressed as a wedding cake in the show Taste, *produced by Chipping Norton Theatre. Costume designed by Nina Ayres.*

Briony and Titania, the fairy queen, in The Rude Mechanical Theatre Company's *adaptation of* A Midsummer Night's Dream.

109

'We use the same pageant wagon every show. It's only really in the costumes that design varies. Like everything else the costumes are "cartoonised", using clown-length trousers, rag or rope wigs, bright colours etc. We only use iconic props (i.e. props that have a purpose over and above their practical function such as teddy bears to suggest innocence). Everything else is mimed. Plus, of course, the battoccio or slapstick, which is a key traditional tool. All music and sound is performed live. We don't use electricity at all, except where we don't have a choice.'

(Pete Talbot, artistic director,
The Rude Mechanical Theatre Company)

Performers at the International Festival of the Sea in hired costumes. Designed by Julia Knight, Portsmouth, 2005.
(Photo: Julia Knight.)

type of hire company you choose will probably be determined by your budget. Institutions like the Royal Shakespeare Company in Stratford, the National Theatre in London and some regional theatres have well-stocked hire departments. Many small towns have theatres with a more limited stock and will hire for a relatively small charge.

All hire companies will issue a bill for any items that have been damaged or require extensive repair work on their return. It's important to tell the hire company that the clothing or props are going to be used outdoors. Many hire companies have particularly prized items that might easily be ruined by the weather or outdoor conditions. For example, if the production requires period clothing, these tend to have long skirts and trains that can quickly become sodden and muddied.

Adapting the costume

If it's not possible to find the exact element required, then the easiest option – other than making it– is to find something approximating its function and to adapt it. This works well in

Handy hint

When making a costume for outdoor theatre that needs to have a full-length skirt, it is a good idea to incorporate a band or frill of a non-absorbent, wipe-clean fabric such as plastic at the hem. This will stop any water on the ground from gradually seeping up the skirt. Likewise, when a train is required in a costume, it is wise to stitch a plastic lining into the underside to protect it from dirt and water. These techniques could be adapted to hired or borrowed costumes, but make sure that only tacking stitches are used to avoid permanently marking the original fabric of the garment.

Generic costume design for street people in The Festival of Christmas, *Historic Dockyard, Portsmouth, 2000. Costume design by Nicola Fitchett.*

productions with large casts, as it's not always possible to make every costume and prop from scratch. It is a good idea to design a generic costume for 'groups' of characters in plays with large casts rather than for each individual character. This will ultimately allow more freedom to adapt pre-existing and 'off the peg' items.

Costumes can be easily adapted by removing elements, sewing on extra pieces of fabric or taking them up or in. If a colour scheme is used in a production, it may be cheaper and easier to dye the fabric rather than buy the costumes new. A certain amount of ingenuity is involved in adapting costumes and it is a time for designers to put their creative thinking to the test.

Performer in Colway Theatre Trust's production On the Green Rock, *wearing a costume made from curtains, gold braid, an 1980s gold belt, some chain and tassels from an old pair of curtain tiebacks.*

Breaking down

'Breaking down' is the term for turning new clothing into something that either looks like it's from a particular period or has been well worn. Adding holes and dirt marks can turn even the simplest of items into convincing and textured period clothing. For a detailed discussion on breaking down, *see* Chapter 8 (page 129).

Where to shop

Pound shops, fancy dress and general bric-a-brac shops sell all manner of plastic and wooden items. Although they may appear unsuitable at first, many items can be transformed when painted with acrylics or metallic paints, or glazed, varnished or given a different texture. Some towns have a craft bank, which, in return for a small yearly subscription, will allow unlimited access to their stores.

'When designing or making large-scale puppets, consider storage facilities available at the venue. If these are limited or unknown, it is advisable to make the puppet in several sections to allow for disassembly. This of course will also facilitate transportation.'

(Mike Bell, puppet maker)

PUPPETRY

Large puppets

In terms of space, large-scale puppets are perfectly suited to outdoor theatre and their only restrictions are either the budget or the ability of those who create them. A large puppet does not always have to be handheld as it can easily be mounted onto a truck or other motorized vehicle. The size and condition of the perform-

'Hunter' puppet in the process of being made by Mike Bell for Full House Theatre Company's Welsh borderland castles tour.
(Photo: Keith Orton)

'Hunter' puppet is held on a pole high above the performer's head so that it can be seen from a distance. (Photo: Keith Orton)

ance area will probably determine whether this is possible. If the puppet is large and therefore heavy, a designer might also consider the use of wheels to move it around the space.

Large handheld puppets should be made of lightweight materials. The designer also needs to consider the possibility of windy conditions. Puppets that extend high above the puppeteers can become difficult to control when brought into an open space. If this is the case, it may be that several puppeteers are needed to distribute the weight and effectively manoeuvre the body parts. It may also be necessary for a longer rehearsal time, as the puppeteers will

Little cabbage puppets create a strong impression when used en masse in this way.
Minack Theatre. (Photo: Keith Orton)

Central School of Speech and Drama's show A Time Machine, *designed by Nina Ayres in collaboration with design students. Minack Theatre, 2006. (Photo: Keith Orton)*

need to practise working together. Large puppets work particularly well outdoors when viewed from a distance. The benefit of having a large puppet as a character means that it will be clearly seen a long way off.

Small puppets

Small puppets tend not to be used in outdoor productions as often as large ones. This is mainly due to the assumption that they will be lost in the space or missed by the audience. However, small puppets can work effectively when grouped together. It helps if smaller puppets are brightly coloured or designed in colours that act as a contrast to the setting. When designing small puppets, always consider the costume worn by the puppeteer as

this should also act as a contrast in order to maximize the puppet's impact.

Puppets worn as costume

A designer might also create a puppet for a performer to wear like a costume. This has the dual advantage of evenly distributing the weight of the puppet and leaves the performer's hands free to manipulate other parts of the structure. The performer's body doesn't have to be completely encased in the puppet and can be partly clothed to create an overall impression of the character. The performer's clothing may need to act as a contrast in order to make a clear distinction between where the puppet begins and the performer ends.

8   MAKING TECHNIQUES

The elements used in an outdoor theatre production may need to be more robust than those used indoors. The pressures of an uneven surface, hostile weather conditions and the possibility of touring or interaction with physical performance styles can all take their toll. Consequently, any painted surfaces on the set should be varnished with a heavy-duty varnish to protect and seal them. Fabrics and methods of construction should be strong enough to withstand the wind: either to harness it or allow it to pass through the fabric. It is also essential that the materials don't disintegrate in the rain and, preferably, don't soak up too much water. This is especially important when making something that will be handheld by a performer.

It is worth trying out all the scenic elements, large costumes and props outside or in the actual site as soon as they are made. Some adjustments will invariably be needed and you may discover the site affects the element's function in ways that hadn't previously been considered.

BEING IMAGINATIVE

It's important to be inventive and to experiment. Each new costume, prop or puppet requires individual consideration in order that it fulfils its function, or functions, as appropriately as possible. Design interpretation is a skill that combines techniques that have been learned with imaginative thinking. For example, I was once given the task of creating a 5m

(15ft) tall puppet with movable eyes, which had to be manipulated by the person carrying it. The production was a community play and thus we were housed in a workshop with limited equipment and budget, and only local shops for inspiration. The final design involved the use of a painted toilet cistern ball inside a transparent hamster bowl, attached to a wooden baton with strings on either side for the performer to manipulate.

The eyes of a puppet are very important. Always try to find a suitable picture of the kind of eyes you're after. There are fundamental design issues around how to make eyes happy, sad etc., so find out what these principles are before you start.

When designing and making puppets (or props) that require two or more performers, be aware of the director's suggestions for movement. What the director wants the puppet to do and what is actually achievable can differ greatly.

MAKING PROPS AND SETS

Polystyrene
Polystyrene is a great material to use because of its versatility: it's light and strong, and can be carved, heat-sealed, textured and painted to resemble almost any surface. It's also completely recyclable. Polystyrene is available in various densities – higher densities are more expensive so should be used for smaller items that require finer detail. It can be bought in sheet form or cut to specific dimensions.

Chair made entirely from polystyrene for a Central School of Speech and Drama production at the Minack Theatre, 1996.

Alternatively, smaller pieces can easily be stuck together with a special contact adhesive (an ordinary contact adhesive, such as 'Evostik', will heat and melt the polystyrene). It's important not to use oil-based paints with polystyrene, as they heat the polystyrene and can become a fire risk.

Polystyrene can be carved and shaped using a saw, bread knife, wire brush or coarse sandpaper. Once carved into shape, the finished article can be heat-sealed using a heat gun. Toxic fumes are emitted from polystyrene when it's heated so a heat gun should only be used in well-ventilated conditions and a vapour mask should be worn. A layer of acrylic (or other water-based paint) can be applied directly to the surface although it should be applied very thinly as a thick layer tends to flake off.

If you need to replicate another material, various textures can be applied to the surface. PVA glue mixed with powder colour or acrylic can be applied more thickly than acrylic alone. A filler, such as sand, gravel or wood shavings, can also be added to the mix to create a good surface texture. It's advisable to add a flame-proofing liquid (such as Flambar) to the final layer of surface decoration as non-porous products don't lend themselves to a liquid or spray.

As an alternative to heating the surface, it's possible to layer the surface with papier-mâché, muslin or other cloths dipped in PVA glue. This will give the piece a smooth finish and create a good surface on which to apply a paint technique. It's also possible to create a textured surface using plaster, although this does have a tendency to chip and flake.

Idendon or stagecoat

Idendon, also known as stagecoat, is a type of plaster used for decoration and texturing on flexible surfaces. It is more flexible than normal plaster and can be used on any scenic canvas, stage floor or as an applied surface to most set elements. It's only available in white or grey, but acrylic paint can be mixed with it to create any colour desired. 'Rosco' paints are particularly good for this, as they are supersaturated and therefore concentrated enough to change the colour of the idendon with just a small amount. Idendon can be applied directly to polystyrene or onto the layer of papier-mâché or fabric with PVA glue. A more intense colour can be achieved by applying a French enamel varnish onto the dried idendon.

Fake leather and metallic costumes

Any costume can be given a fake leather look with the application of idendon, although it's advisable to use a heavy-duty fabric such as canvas or drill if the garment is being made up specifically for this treatment.

Idendon, mixed with acrylic paint, should ideally be applied to the fabric using an artist's palette knife. Once this layer is dry, a layer of French enamel varnish should be applied. Finally, after the French enamel has fully dried, a shoe polish should be rubbed into the surface and allowed to soak in for a couple of minutes. The article can then be buffed with a soft cloth for a 'leather look' shine. A metallic effect can be achieved on practically any surface simply by applying a metallic paint (such as 'rub'n'buff') to the dried layer of idendon.

Design for a puppet of Napoleon Bonaparte for The International Festival of The Sea, 2005. (Source: Nina Ayres)

Plastazote

Plastazote is a dense foam, which can be cut and sculpted much like a dress pattern to create all manner of costumes, puppets and props. It is an excellent material to use in outdoor theatre, as it's light and waterproof. It is supplied in sheet form (approximately one metre in width and two metres in length) and comes in various thicknesses. It is easily cut with ordinary craft scissors, while neater edges can be achieved with a scalpel and cutting mat. Edges can be glued together with an ordinary contact adhesive. Always ensure that the glue is spread evenly and thinly to each surface and allowed to dry to a tacky finish before bringing the two surfaces together.

Make sure you choose the right thickness of Plastazote. As a general rule, large items will

Making Humpty Dumpty puppets using Plastazote for a Central School of Speech and Drama production entitled The Quest *at the Minack Theatre, 2005. (Photo: Keith Orton)*

need a piece that is at least 8mm (½in) thick in order to have some rigidity. Plastazote is also available in tube form. This can be treated in the same way as the sheet form and is particularly useful in creating raised patterns and ridges on sculptured garments.

Painting Plastazote

Plastazote isn't an easy surface to paint as it has the same soft properties as polystyrene and paint tends to chip or peel. Very diluted acrylic paints can create light colours on Plastazote if they are worked well into the surface. A Plastazote primer is available to enable ordinary acrylic or aerosol paints to be applied, but it's expensive and has some toxic qualities. To create a surface to paint on, attach layers of paper or muslin strips and PVA glue to the outer edge (this also adds a harder shell to the piece). In fact, any of the techniques used to create textures on polystyrene, including the use of idendon, can be easily adapted for Plastazote.

USING WHEELS

In making wheels, you need to consider the surface on which the object will be moving. It is always important to check the load bearing capacity of any wheel and to ensure that the object, including any people who might be sitting or standing in it, does not exceed this. On a turf or earth flooring, thin wheels can become incredibly difficult to move and can easily get stuck after a small amount of rain. Wide 'cart' wheels are the most appropriate kind for performance areas with grass or earth flooring.

Swivel wheels

Plastic swivel wheels come in a variety of shapes and sizes and with a range of load-bearing capabilities. They are better at handling uneven surfaces and many can be locked

The puppet Napoleon sitting on his horse made from withy and tissue paper over a strong wooden base, which is mounted to a steel frame with wheels.

Handy hint

When creating large forms in a workshop, always be aware of the size of the exit. You may well be creating something that won't be able to get through the doors of the workshop in one piece. In the picture above, Napoleon was 6m (20ft) tall and had to be designed with a 'hinged section' across his body so that he could safely exit the 3m (10ft) doors of the workshop.

in to position. However, they are difficult to control if there is any kind of rake and it might be better to use a 'non-swivel' variety. An ideal solution is to attach swivel wheels to the front and fixed wheels to the back. This will enable the piece to turn corners more easily and prevents the back from swinging out.

Bicycle wheels

Bicycle wheels can work well but do have a few drawbacks. They aren't particularly strong and have a low load-bearing threshold. They are also prone to puncturing, unlike solid wood or plastic wheels, and when attached to a solid frame, turn corners with difficulty. Ensure that the wheels aren't permanently welded to the frame and can be removed if the inner tube needs changing.

Puppet on wheels

The advantage of securing a puppet onto a vehicle or on wheels is that its weight will be evenly distributed. It can be heavier than a handheld puppet and can include materials that harness the wind. How feasible this is depends on the size and scale of the piece, so it's a good idea to consult with an engineer or someone who is experienced at making larger puppets and to talk through the design.

SCALING UP

Scaling up is useful for elements that need to be built to a bigger size than the available template will allow. The Humpty Dumpty models shown on page 118 were made by this method. The construction of Humpty Dumpty involved an original egg shape, which was then moulded from Plastazote, using the following process.

The scaling up technique suggested here can be applied to most objects, although more complicated shapes may need to be made in several sections. If this is the case, put pattern

A practical example of scaling up

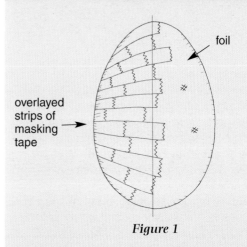

foil

overlayed strips of masking tape

Figure 1

1. A foil-wrapped Easter egg was entirely covered in small strips of masking tape (Figure 1).
2. The central seam was then marked with pen and the 'mould' (foil and masking tape) cut away from the egg with a scalpel, leaving two identical halves (Figure 2).

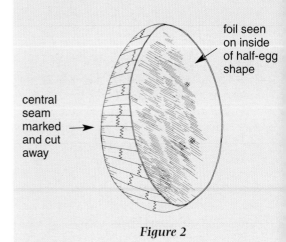

foil seen on inside of half-egg shape

central seam marked and cut away

Figure 2

A practical example of scaling up

3. The height of the egg was measured and a ratio worked out as to how many times bigger the 'real' thing would have to be. (For example, my model egg measured 10″ and I wanted to create a finished product 40″ in height, so the ratio was 1:4; that is, the finished product was to be four times bigger than the original.)

4. One half of the mould then had incisions cut into the sides until the shape lay completely flat.

5. This shape was then traced on to a piece of paper marked out with a grid of 1″ squares (Figure 3). A large piece of paper was then laid out and squares marked on in accordance to the ratio needed. So my ratio had been worked out as 1:4, therefore the large piece of paper needed to have 4″ squares marked onto it. A scaled-up version of the smaller drawing was then drawn onto the large sheet of paper and cut out.

6. This large pattern piece was then attached to the sheet of 4mm Plastazote and spraymount used to keep it in place. A scalpel was used to cut each seam at a neat 90 degree angle to ensure a smooth finish and the paper pattern peeled carefully away from the Plastazote (Figure 4).

7. Each incision was then glued together with contact adhesive before the second half was cut, in case any amendments needed to be made to the shape (Figure 5).

8. Finally the second half was cut and glued to the first half to create the perfect egg shape which then had leg holes and decoration added.

the finished template is then laid onto a 1″ squared grid

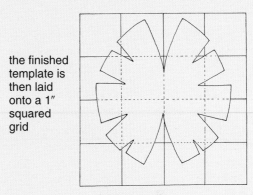

Figure 3

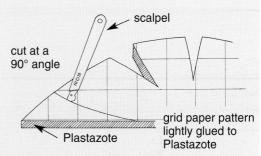

scalpel

cut at a 90° angle

grid paper pattern lightly glued to Plastazote

Plastazote

Figure 4

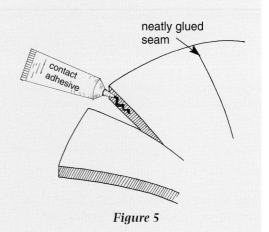

neatly glued seam

contact adhesive

Figure 5

Goosey Goosey Gander puppet made entirely from Plastazote and powernet. The feathers are made from sculpted Plastazote, attached to the body. **The Quest, Minack Theatre, 2005.** *(Photo: Keith Orton)*

'Mock-ups' can be made from card and used to take pattern pieces from, or an experienced craftsperson can create the desired shape from trial and error.

Combining techniques

Sometimes, scaling up requires the combination of other techniques. The goose (see illustration) was made in a more ad hoc way and used extensively in rehearsals before being altered and adjusted. The neck and head sections were made from Plastazote and mounted onto a hardhat to give the head left and right movement. The lower part of the neck piece was made from powernet, which enabled the performer to see and breathe with ease. This also created a surface on which to attach the feathers.

The goose's feathers were made from Plastazote. The Plastazote was cut into feather shapes and then the spine detail and separations 'burnt' into the Plastazote using a soldering iron. A soldering iron will melt Plastazote so that it shrinks and creates indentations in the surface. The feathers were then heated with a heat gun and held in curves until the Plastazote cooled. This technique created the natural curl typical of feathers.

Please note that melting Plastazote creates toxic fumes and should only be done in well-ventilated areas and wearing a vapour mask.

WITHY LANTERNS AND WET-STRENGTH TISSUE PAPER

Many outdoor shows that extend into the night use withy and tissue paper structures with some kind of light inside to create a lantern effect. Traditionally, this light would be emitted from a tea light or candle secured to the base but many companies now use small battery-operated lights. This removes the risk

markings, also known as balance points, across the lines that will be cut to separate the pieces and number them for easy reference. Sometimes the scaled-up pattern will be larger than one sheet of Plastazote, so glue the edges of the Plastazote together. Always remove the shiny edges of the Plastazote before attaching them as they don't bond well and will, consequently, be less strong. However, it's not always necessary to scale up in this way.

of the candles going out or setting fire to the lantern. If candles or tea lights are used, the lantern should first be treated with a flame-proofed layer, there should always be a fire extinguisher nearby, and the performer holding the lantern should be wearing non-flammable clothing. Withy lanterns are usually pyramid shaped, since they're easy to construct, and create a stunning effect when seen en masse. Instructions for making withy lanterns are given on pages 124 and 125.

Withy

Withy, or willow, is a natural reed that can be bought cheaply. When soaked in water, it is extremely flexible and can be bent into various shapes. Alternatively, several reeds can be attached together with small pieces of thin wire. Masking tape can be used to attach straight pieces of dry withy but will slip away from wet withy, especially when the reed is bent at an angle. You should bear this in mind in case of wet weather.

Wet-strength tissue paper

Wet-strength tissue paper differs from ordinary tissue paper in that it retains its shape and strength when wet. This is important as a mixture of PVA glue and water is sponged onto the tissue paper prior to being attached to the outside of the withy structure. Make sure you cut each piece of tissue to the required size and let all the pieces on one side of the structure dry before turning it over to apply tissue on the opposite side. This will prevent pieces from falling off when the structure is turned. The PVA and water mix should always be applied on a non-porous surface, such as laminate or plastic sheeting, and the sponging action directed from the middle of the sheet to the outside. This will enable the tissue to stretch slightly and dry taut on the lantern structure.

It's possible to create all manner of shapes and creatures by building the withies in

Large lantern ship being constructed using rattan for The Sailor Horse, Minehead *community play by Claque Theatre Company, formerly Colway Theatre Company. (Photo: Jon Oram)*

sculptured forms and then covering them with tissue paper.

The technique can be taken even further and used to make large, lightweight structures that can easily be worn by a performer.

It's not always necessary to cover the withies in tissue paper. Withies used on their own can create strong forms with an organic feel.

Attaching wadding or fabric to withies can also create an unusual effect. Fabric can be applied directly to a withy structure using 'copydex' glue or wrapped around individual sticks as a way of colouring the structure.

Making withy lanterns

Tools and materials

Secateurs or wire cutters; ten lengths of willow (roughly 1.5–2m each), soaked overnight in water; five sheets of wet strength tissue paper; tape measure; scissors; sponge; PVA glue and water mix (ratio 3:2); thin wire; a light source, such as a tea light or small battery-operated light; non-porous surface such as laminate or perspex.

Method

1. Use a pair of secateurs or wire cutters to cut the lengths of willow into ten identical lengths (roughly 50-100cm) and put the remaining pieces back into the water. Make a square from four of the identical sticks by tying the ends together with wire (Figure 1). This will form the base of the lantern.

2. Attach another identical piece of willow to each of the corners of the base, bringing them together to form a pyramid shape. Use the remaining two pieces of willow to create a cross in the centre by attaching them to either side (Figure 2).

3. The structure is then ready to be strengthened using the remaining willow that has been left to soak. Create patterns over the frame or randomly attach the willow lengths, remembering to leave a space large enough to get your hand through on one of the sides (Figure 3). This will later be used as a door to give access to the light source.

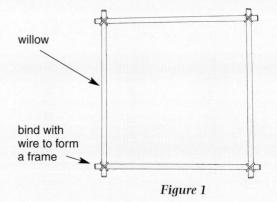

willow

bind with wire to form a frame

Figure 1

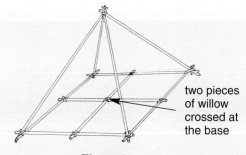

two pieces of willow crossed at the base

Figure 2

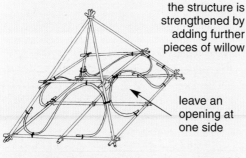

the structure is strengthened by adding further pieces of willow

leave an opening at one side

Figure 3

4. The structure is now ready to have the wet-strength tissue paper applied. Working on one side at a time, measure and cut the tissue paper to fit, allowing a small overlap on each side. Dip a sponge into the PVA-water mix and squeeze out the excess. Place the cut out tissue onto the non-porous surface and, working from the centre of each sheet, spread the glue mix onto the tissue before position-

Making withy lanterns

ing it into place on the willow frame. Repeat this process on two more sides, leaving the opening for the door and the base (Figure 4).

5. Make a door frame shape using small pieces of left-over willow. Cover the door in tissue paper in the same manner as the lantern. The structure and the door should then be left to dry before attach-

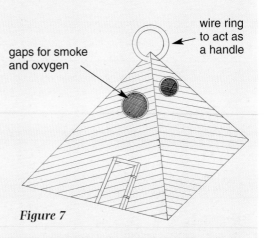

Figure 7

stretch the glued tissue over the frame, allowing a slight overlap at each edge

opening for door

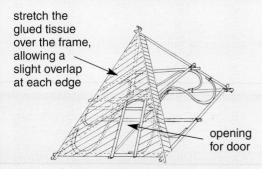

Figure 4

wire loops act as hinges

door

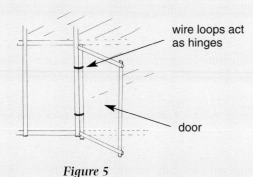

Figure 5

willow cross

wire to hold tea light secure

tea light base

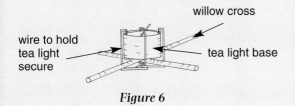

Figure 6

ing the door to one side of the frame by way of wire loops acting as 'door hinges' (Figure 5).

6. The light is then ready to be wired to the central base of the lantern. This can be done by removing a tea light from its base, then pushing wire through the metal, and wrapping the wire around the cross of willow until it is secure (Figure 6). The tea light can then be popped back into its base. If an electric light is to be used, it can be wired directly to the central cross bar of the base, making sure that no wire covers the power switch.

7. Finally the base can be covered with wet-strength tissue paper in the same manner as the sides, and the whole structure allowed to dry.

8. Lastly, push a length of wire through the tissue paper at the top of the lantern to make a loop. This can act as a handle, either hand-held or attached to a long piece of bamboo for carrying high above the performer's head. If a tea light candle has been used, small holes will need to be cut near the top of the lantern to let oxygen in and smoke out (Figure 7).

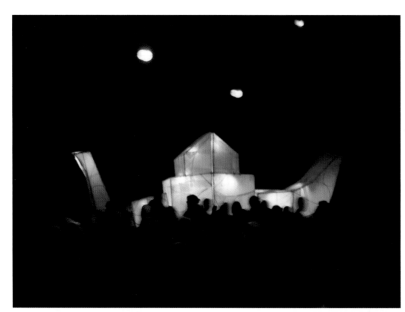

Different abstract-shaped lanterns coming together to form a Venetian barge when carried in above the heads of a promenade audience. Made for the Tonbridge community play **The Jealous River** *by the Claque Theatre Company. (Photo: Jon Oram)*

Lantern element to the closing ceremony of the Commonwealth Games by Walk the Plank. (Photo: Walk the Plank)

Puppet made using withies by Mike Bell and students from the Central School of Speech and Drama for a production of Merlin's Child *at the Minack Theatre, 2006.* (Photo: Keith Orton)

CREATING LARGE OR LIGHTWEIGHT STRUCTURES

Wire mesh

Both chicken wire and lightweight aluminium mesh, available from sculpting suppliers, can be used to create large structures. Chicken wire is relatively inexpensive and can be used for larger objects that don't require intricate detail. Aluminium mesh is lighter and more closely woven than chicken wire, and can be cut to shape with scissors and used to make more detailed pieces. Bear in mind that any hollow structures made using these materials and techniques will never be strong enough to be sat on or stood on. However, they are perfect for sculpted forms intended to viewed, not interacted with.

Lord Fish designed by Nicola Fitchett for the International Festival of the Sea, 2001. (Photo: Nicola Fitchett)

Lord and Lady Fish, head designs interpreted by Jon Saunders using an aluminium mesh base with layered tissue paper and PVA glue.

Covering the mesh

After the shape or design is constructed, a covering is then applied. Covering the structure with PVA and wet strength tissue paper will give it a translucent look but do remember the shape of the wire will show through. However, this is particularly useful for masks or headpieces as performers will be able to see through the tissue.

Papier-mâché attached with PVA glue will create a denser finish than tissue paper, and muslin attached with PVA glue will be even stronger and denser. Various other fabrics coated in copydex can be applied directly to the mesh, and wadding can be inserted between the wire mesh and fabric for a smoother finish. A similar effect can also be achieved by using cardboard to build up the structure, with wadding glued in place to shape the piece. The entire structure will then need to be covered in strips of muslin, or other thin cotton fabric, and copydex to bond everything together.

Using copydex also means the structure will now be waterproof, so any pieces made in this way are safe to be used outdoors.

HEADPIECES

If the production requires outsized hats, wigs, or any headpiece that cannot be built from an initial structure, Plastazote can be used to create the base, and then fabric or fake hair added for decoration. This is a very effective way to make large or outsized headpieces as the finished product is incredibly light and comfortable to wear. Start by shaping the Plastazote and then attach the fabric using a contact adhesive. Thick fabric is preferable, as it doesn't allow the glue to seep through, which may potentially mark the surface. It's important that the Plastazote is bent into its finished shape before the fabric is attached. If the fabric is attached beforehand it will stop the Plastazote from bending outwards; conversely,

Star mask made by Bonnie Corbett under instruction from Julian Crouch of Improbable Theatre for a production at the Central School of Speech and Drama, 1996. (Photo: Bonnie Corbett)

Three of the finished Star masks, created by layering wadding, muslin and copydex glue over a fabric base. (Photo: Julia Knight)

the fabric will wrinkle untidily if the Plastazote is then bent inwards. The finished headpiece can be mounted onto a tight-fitting skullcap – which can also be made of Plastazote – a cycle helmet or a hard hat to help it stay firmly in place.

Cycle helmets and hard hats form excellent bases for any piece of set or props worn as headgear. They are particularly useful when their plastic coating is removed, exposing the high-density foam inside. This can then be used rather like a florist's 'oasis', allowing wire to be pushed directly into it so that items can be attached to the top.

The wire mesh technique mentioned above can also be used for creating lightweight structures to be worn as headdresses.

BREAKING DOWN TECHNIQUES

Breaking down, as mentioned in Chapter 7 (*see* page 112), is simply the technique of making elements in the production appear worn or used. It's always important to 'age'

Large wigs under construction in the workshop at the International Festival of the Sea, 2005. The wigs were made by Enda Kenny using a Plastazote base with synthetic hair glued in place. (Photo: Julia Knight)

scenic elements and costumes in order to create wholly realistic characters and settings. Careful consideration is necessary for each element and the extent of breaking down will obviously vary.

Breaking down for set and props can be a simple matter of using spray paints to create a dirty effect in corners or along the hems of fabric. Alternatively, a plastic spray bottle can be filled with a watered-down brown acrylic paint and sprayed directly onto any surface. Fabrics can easily be aged by creating holes with a cheese grater or by sandpapering. They can also be 'dip dyed' to take away the freshness of a colour or have acrylic paint 'dry brushed' onto the surface to give the impression of ground-in dirt. Talcum powder and 'Fullers Earth' are both effective for creating a dusty look. 'Tulip' fabric paints are available in dull metallic finishes and can be applied to shiny metallic fastenings to dull them. For a longer lasting effect, black metal grate polish can also be used to take the shine off any metal work.

'A word of warning about dyeing fabric that is going to be used as outdoor scenery. Fix those dyes really well – better than you would usually. We learnt this to our cost in torrential rains when brightly coloured laundry lines flapping overhead began to drip, and disgruntled audience members complained about orange spots on their clothes.

(Nicola Fitchett, freelance designer)

MAKING FLAGS

'Ripstop' is a strong, lightweight fabric, which is particularly good at harnessing the wind. It can be used to make flags or windsocks in a variety of shapes and sizes. Another advantage of ripstop is that it can be glued together with PVA, rather than sewn, which makes it a good material for workshops with children.

It's important to remember the design of any piece if it needs to be easily viewed by the audience. Complicated designs, or text written on the fabric, may not work if the wind either blows in the wrong direction or doesn't blow at all.

RAGGING

Ragging is the technique of attaching strips of cloth closely together onto a base fabric. Outdoor theatre often uses ragging in its

The Ancient Mariner, here seen with his albatross, shows the extent of breaking down needed to create realistic costumes and props.

Windsocks made from brightly coloured ripstop by members of the community cast at the International Festival of the Sea, 2001.

costumes, especially for pagan celebrations and mummers' plays. If the budget is tight, strips of fabric are an inexpensive way of creating colourful costumes with a lot of movement and texture. Traditionally these garments would have had each piece of fabric sewn on individually, but now 'kimble tag' guns are commonly used as they are inexpensive and quickly attach cloth to cloth.

When choosing a fabric, remember that natural fabrics can become very heavy when wet and may take a long time to dry out. Substituting lightweight synthetic fabrics will alleviate this problem: netting or tulle is ideal, and even plastic carrier bags or black refuse sacks can be used to create a lightweight costume.

BODY PADDING

Body padding is traditionally achieved using either shaped wadding or foam, which can be then stitched into the performer's costume if required. This type of padding isn't ideal for an outdoor production as foam or wadding acts as a sponge and becomes heavy and difficult to dry out when wet. For outdoor theatre, netting or tulle is ideal for use in creating body shapes as it is much more lightweight and also dries more quickly. The netting or tulle can have fabric strips attached to the outer edge to keep a ruffled appearance or garments can be worn directly over it in the same way as padding.

Making tulle net body padding

Tools and materials

Lycra body stocking that closely fits the performer; tailor's chalk; scissors; spandex; tulle netting; iron; needle and thread; sewing machine.

Method

1. Using tailor's chalk, mark on the body stocking the sections that require padding (Figure 1).
2. Cut away the marked sections and use them as patterns to cut pieces from a heavy-duty spandex fabric, allowing 1cm all round for a seam (Figure 2).
3. Chalk horizontal lines roughly 2cm apart on the spandex pieces.
4. Cut pieces of tulle netting into long strips of various widths, ranging in width from roughly 5–11cm. Each strip should then be folded in half lengthways and ironed in order to create a central spine.
5. Using the chalk lines for guidance, attach the pieces of tulle to the spandex pieces in order of width, using the 5cm strips at either end of the spandex section, and using longer pieces the closer you get to the centre (Figure 3). Each strip is attached by opening out the fold in the tulle and using the crease as a marking for the sewing line. Using a stretch stitch

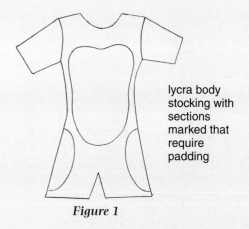

lycra body stocking with sections marked that require padding

Figure 1

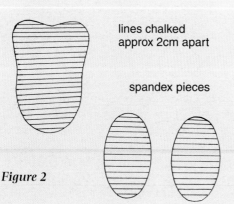

lines chalked approx 2cm apart

spandex pieces

Figure 2

spandex piece

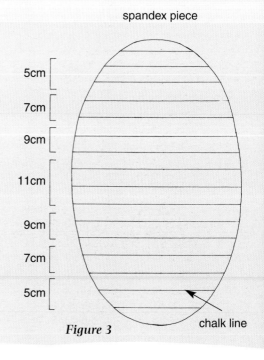

5cm

7cm

9cm

11cm

9cm

7cm

5cm

chalk line

Figure 3

Making tulle net body padding

on a sewing machine such as zigzag, or three-step zigzag, sew the tulle along the chalked lines on the spandex pieces. As you sew, push more net under the foot of the sewing machine in order to create a ruffled effect to the tulle net (Figure 4). The tulle should stop short of the 1cm seam allowance.

stitch along the centre of the tulle strips, using the chalk lines for guidance

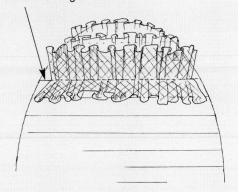

Figure 4

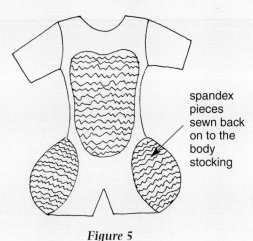

spandex pieces sewn back on to the body stocking

Figure 5

6. The spandex with attached strips of tulle can then be sewn into place on the body-suit effectively replacing the lycra sections which were initially cut out (Figure 5). These are best sewn into place using an overlocker. If an overlocker is not available, they can be sewn into place using a strong zigzag stitch (it is wise to tack the piece into position before attempting this on the sewing machine).

7. The finished product should then be placed on the performer or a mannequin and the whole thing shaped to the desired finish. This shaping is done by hand using an ordinary pair of scissors and concentrates on blending the net-ting into the body shape, thus making the padding flow seamlessly over the entire body.

8. If the garment is a fur suit or is not to be worn under clothing, then the body padding lycra bodysuit will have fabric attached directly to it to act as a costume. 5cm strips of fabric or fur can be added to the outer edge of each piece of tulle (Figure 6), holding them in place with a kimble tag gun. This will enable the tulle sections to blend in with the overall gar-ment, and will also allow each piece of tulle to move independently. This will give the performer maximum flexibility and allow air to circulate, thus making it much more comfortable than conven-tional padding.

kimble tags

fabric/fur strips

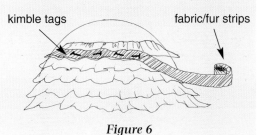

Figure 6

9 PRACTICAL CONSIDERATIONS OF THE SPACE

PUBLIC AMENITIES

A company needs to be aware of the welfare of its performers and audience and take the necessary steps to ensure that everyone is catered for. The first consideration should be the public amenities available in and around the site. A company must remember that its audience needs to access the site with as much ease as possible. Start by identifying where the audience might reasonably travel from and check that there are bus or train links. Don't forget to check the times of the last buses or trains and time the show accordingly. The easier it is for an audience to get to the space, the more chance you have of increased attendance.

If the venue has no public transport, a company may decide to offer a shuttle service from the nearby towns and villages. Obviously this may have budget implications, which some companies will be unlikely to afford. An alternative that is known to work is to come to an agreement with a local taxi firm who will offer discounts to anyone wishing to see the show.

Car parking

The most common mode of transport to outdoor venues is by car, and a company should always make sure there is sufficient car park-

'People bring their own garden chairs or rugs. We rope off the central aisle and sightlines. We have a risk assessment, which is brought up to date every year. It's used as a model for outdoor theatre by two different district councils. We have fire-fighting equipment. Our shows have to have public loos and adequate parking nearby. The site arrangements allow a fast get-in (an hour) and get-out (45 minutes). We don't usually arrive until 4.00pm for a show at 7.30pm.'

(Pete Talbot,
The Rude Mechanical Theatre Company)

ing space available. If the venue is in a built-up area, check whether there are parking restrictions during the playing time of the production. If so, guide the audience to car parks in the vicinity. If there are just a few parking spaces available, prioritize these for disabled drivers. Don't forget to check the closing times of the car parks you may have sent people to and make sure the production finishes well before. All this information should be made available to audience members prior to the production, either on the web or enclosed with the tickets.

A sculpture set up to help mark the route along which the audience should travel, Souterrain *by WildWorks, Stanmer Park, 2005.*

A shrine set up along the path which the audience should take, Souterrain *by WildWorks, 2005.*

Creating a car park

If the production is taking place in a remote location, it may be necessary to create a temporary car park. It's crucial to have attendants on hand to direct people since the area will not be marked and most people try to park as near as possible to the entrance, which always creates problems. Bear in mind the suitability of the area. Mostly it will be grass, but it's important to make sure the surface remains intact, even in wet weather. It's not uncommon for cars to become stuck, especially if the area has been used over a period of days.

Make some contingency plans in the event of bad weather. Have some bales of straw on hand to spread over the entrance and exit areas and, if possible, have a 4×4 vehicle, complete with towrope, on standby to pull vehicles from the mud. Make sure there's a suitable amount of space set aside for disabled or elderly audience members. If the journey from the car park to the performance area requires some navigation, clearly signpost how to get to the site or position ushers along the route.

Making the car park part of the performance

As mentioned previously, some companies actually make the car park a part of the event itself. Some productions give the stewards costumes or characters to play, whilst others station musicians along the route. Rather than employ standard signposting, some companies use installations and sculptures to guide the audiences to the playing area. If access to the site is particularly treacherous, it's important that the audience, especially the disabled and the elderly, are made aware. Once again, post this information on the web or include it with the tickets.

Using volunteers

Companies often employ the services of local volunteers to help steward an event. There is a variety of youth organizations, such as scout or cadet groups, which will help steward a production, especially if offered a free viewing of the show. For legal reasons, there must be an appropriate number of stewards who have been fully briefed of their role. They should also be clearly identifiable, even if they are in costumes or playing a character.

Toilets

Also crucial to an audience's welfare is the provision of a public toilet. Although there may already be one available at the site – in a

public park, for example – permission should be sought to use it before, during and after the production. It's important to check if there is access to it at all times. If it is usually locked at a certain hour, the key-keeper may require additional payment to keep it open for longer. Don't take the use of a toilet for granted: if ignored, a minor point such as this can become a major issue on the day.

If there are no public toilets on site, or permission to use them cannot be obtained, then portable toilets can be hired. The hire company will advise on the number needed for the size of your event. In the height of the summer season, portable toilets are in popular demand so it's advisable to book these as soon as the site and performance dates have been set.

Water

Portable toilets require the use of water. The catering may require water and the production may use water during the show. If there are no suitable water facilities nearby, then

Wardens are clearly visible in waistcoats with light reflectors at a production of The Bell *by Periplum and the World Famous in Alexandra Park, Hastings. (Photo: Deborah Pearson)*

The Nelson's Arm public bar was set up temporarily for the International Festival of the Sea, Portsmouth, 2005. It held regular 'cock fights', performed on the forecourt, to keep the public entertained.

tanks of water, sometimes referred to as water bowsers, will need to be hired and appropriate pipes laid.

Catering and box office

Catering is not necessary to a production, although it can be a good way of creating extra revenue, especially if a premises licence, which permits the sale of alcohol, is obtained. A bar can work as a place to keep the audience contained before the show and, if it's covered, as a shelter in the event of a downpour. Events that are planned to take place during colder times of year may offer simple drinks like tea, soup and mulled wine. The bar can be themed in keeping with the play, or have entertain-

ment of its own, before, during or after the event to make the experience more integrated.

The company will have to provide rubbish bins and to hire a skip if large numbers of people are expected to attend. If no catering or bar service is made available, and the audience is relatively small, companies are perfectly within their rights to ask people to take their rubbish with them at the end of the show.

A paid event will require a box office, where the audience can purchase or collect tickets, buy programmes and make any general enquiries about the production. It's always advisable for the box office to have plenty of change and a torch to guide late-comers into the space. If the site has more than one

Tents on either side of the stage act as 'quick-change' areas for the cast. The Princess, the Palace and the Ice Cold Bath, 2006.

entrance or exit, front of house staff or stewards should be appointed to guide the audience to the appropriate area.

AMENITIES FOR THE CAST AND CREW

It may be necessary to find local accommodation for the crew and performers, and this will need to be budgeted for. Many community plays will ask members of the cast to house the crew while working on the production. It's also common for local bed and breakfasts or hotels to accommodate the whole cast and crew for a particular length of time. If a block booking can be made, then it's usual to pay less than the standard room rate. Some established theatres also have a 'digs' list, which can usually be obtained in advance.

Washing facilities

A wardrobe department will always need to know where the nearest washing facilities are.

If possible, the production manager should secure their use on site. Alternatively, he/she should find out the opening hours of the nearest launderette and ensure that time is allowed in the schedule for any necessary washing. Some actors prefer to take small items of their costume back to their accommodation to wash. This approach works well, so long as the actors and crew are clear that this is the established procedure.

Offstage facilities

The offstage facilities required by performers and crew are similar to those of the audience. Access to a toilet and a dressing room is essential. The performers will need a place to change into costume both before and during the show. If possible, there should be one area for men, another for women and a separate changing room for any children in the cast. The performers and crew should be provided with safe drinking water and if possible, tea- and coffee-making facilities.

Making the area safe

Hazardous entrance points should be made safe. Handrails should be erected for uneven steps, and dark areas in the space should have some lighting. It is far too easy for performers to trip or hurt themselves whilst rushing to get on stage, especially if they're on tour and have to contend with different offstage areas. Likewise, the stage or acting area should be free from any trip hazards, and if a raised platform is used, the edge of the stage must be clearly marked.

Keeping a kit bag

In case something needs repairing, each department should make sure it has a kit bag with the necessary equipment. It's a good idea to have a spare item of anything that has the potential to break. Items such as cable ties, fuses, knives, wire, glue, string, matting, gaffer or LX tape and general sewing equipment are essential items in any kit bag. Regardless of whether or not the production is in a remote place away from shops, these items will inevitably be needed at some point.

Mobile phones

You may find that mobile phones don't work in the space so check the site beforehand. Walkie-talkies are an excellent alternative and a good investment generally, as they enable communication between the technical and creative staff on site and allow information to be heard by everyone.

TECHNICAL CONSIDERATIONS

Lighting

If the production starts early, there is every possibility that lighting will not have to be used at all. But should you require lighting for part, or all of the production, there are a number of solutions that can be explored depending on the budget.

Lighting without electricity

If it isn't possible to use electricity in the space, there are alternative solutions. Naked flames, such as torches, can be used as long as safety procedures are met. Often pyrotechnics, fireworks and light sculptures form much of the actual show and therefore negate the need for additional lighting. On a more low-key note, battery-operated, solar-powered, wind-up or rechargeable lamps can be used to light up pathways or small pieces of action, especially when held by the performers. The Globe Theatre's touring production of *Romeo and Juliet* used solar-powered garden lights to mark the path to the car park and the tour van's headlights to illuminate the exit.

The Rude Mechanical Theatre Company uses butane gas canisters with lanterns rigged on top, which produces a floodlit effect similar to that of road works at night. They may not be theatrically perfect, but lanterns do the job of lighting the second half of the show. They are in fact an excellent solution to the challenges of The Rude Mechanical Theatre Company's long summer tour. The Company performs at a different venue each night and, consequently, needs to be self-sufficient. By using gas canisters, it isn't reliant on an electricity supply and can execute a very quick get in and get out.

Using a generator

Some venues will require a power supply to light the production or surrounding area. If the site is particularly remote, then a generator may need to be sourced. Generators can be hired to fulfil almost any power task, and hire companies will advise on what's suitable for the production's requirements. Bigger productions often have a generator on standby in the event of an emergency, and it's possible to link two generators so that if one fails, the other automatically takes over. Hire companies now supply a range of generators that are silent, so

139

The butane gas lamps used to light the Rude Mechanical Theatre Company's shows are clearly seen in the foreground.

avoiding problems of noise. Generators can emit fumes and should be placed as far away as possible from the action. Take note of the wind direction so it carries any fumes away from the actors, catering and audience.

Types of lights
If a company chooses to use theatre lanterns, they will either have to be purchased or hired for the duration of the production. There are generally four types of lantern that are used in theatre productions, and each has its unique qualities.

Parcans are the most popular lanterns used in outdoor venues, as they have no moving parts or lenses. Bright and fairly robust, they

are relatively cheap in comparison to other lanterns and offer great coverage.

Profiles are ideal if a hard edge is needed to confine a light to a specific spot as they have movable shutters. Gobos can also be attached to give a specific effect or shape to the light.

Fresnels provide a soft pool of light to a general area.

Floodlights flood a large area with a bright light, but offer little theatrical ambiance.

Some productions hire a lighting company with a full technical team to oversee the installation and use of the equipment. Other companies use their own technicians to carry out the installation and oversee the lanterns during the performance.

Richard Delight rigging fresnels and parcans for a show at the Minack Theatre in Cornwall. (Photo: Keith Orton)

Cable protector with rope light contained within to make it more visible in large crowds. Faithless tour 2007. (Photo: Jono Kenyon)

Safety

There have been many recent innovations in outdoor lighting, which have alleviated some of the risks involved in using lights outdoors. 'Ecodomes' are clear, air-filled protection devices that encase the lantern and keep it watertight, even under extreme weather conditions. A company called Airstar makes 'balloon lights' consisting of helium- or air-filled balloons that either drift or can be mounted at any height. These balloons can withstand high winds, rain and even snow and are a safe alternative.

All electrical equipment for use outdoors will have an IP rating. This indicates the equipment's resilience to rain and dust, so the higher the IP rating, the more robust it will be. All electrical equipment used in an outdoor production should be RCD (Residual Current Device) protected, so that in the event of a fault, the power will automatically cut off. Sixteen-amp plugs and sockets called 'ceeform' connections are watertight and specifically designed for the outdoors. It is especially important that the connections between cables are kept as dry as possible: and taping a plastic bag around all connections in bad weather is good practice.

Cables

Any wires required for the lighting and sound should not lie above ground for any length of time because of their susceptibility to damage or waterlogging. Some companies dig trenches to allow the cables to run underground, but this does not protect them entirely and they

The yellow jacket and bumblebee series of hinged-lid cable protectors are widely used at outdoor events.

eventually emerge incredibly muddy. A device called a 'truck track', which has been in use for many years, encases the cables while safely allowing access to them if a fault occurs. This method also means both audience and vehicles can traverse the space without hindrance.

Protecting the equipment

The dimmer racks are the only part of the lighting system that absolutely must be placed under cover. All sorts of structures can be used as cover, from a table with a gazebo over the top, to a scaffold tower covered with tarpaulin on all sides. Whatever structure is chosen to protect the equipment, it's important it has attachable sides to shelter the equipment from horizontal rain. Flight cases (metal cases which are used to transport light and sound equipment) or pallets can be used to raise the equipment off the ground. Specific shelters can be designed for the sound and lighting

areas to blend in with the space, depending on the budget and scale of the production.

A clear view

It's vital that the audience can see and hear the action clearly, regardless of where the lighting and sound operators are located. One of the reasons scaffolding towers are commonly used is because they perform the dual function of housing the operators and equipment, whilst also creating a platform to hang the lamps from. This also means that the operators can be placed in a fairly prominent position without masking the audience's view or attracting attention.

Sound

In an outdoor performance, sound equipment can be used to amplify performers' voices or instruments and enables the playing of pre-recorded music, effects or dialogue. The actual need for sound depends on a variety of factors:

142

Scaffolding erected to hang lights and house the lighting equipment, including dimmer rack and lighting operator. **The Princess, the Palace and the Ice Cold Bath,** *Claremont,* **2006.** *(Photo: Peter Watters)*

the acoustics and size of the space, the strength of the performers' voices and the requirements of the text. If amplification is needed only for specific moments, then a loud hailer can be used.

Sound requires electricity, just as lighting does. It is good practice to keep the sound and lighting equipment separate. If placed together, the dimmer rack, and its electrical supply, can cause the sound to hum or buzz. Consequently, the equipment should also have a separate supply of electricity. Most sound is now run from a computer so it's important to have a UPS (Uninterruptible Power Supply) unit. Should the power fail, this will immediately kick in and prevent the computer from shutting down.

Waterproofing and protection

Waterproof versions of cables and connections are readily available. Alternatively, technicians will often wrap the cables and connections in plastic bags and cover the

Scaffold lighting tower and tent used to house the sound equipment and operator, with waterproof covers to protect the equipment. (Photo: Peter Watters)

***The sound and lighting equipment has been lifted off the floor with bricks.* The Persians,**
Thiasos Theatre Company, Oxford, 2006. *(Photo: Andrew Derrington)*

speakers between performances for extra protection from the wind, dust and rain. If a very large set of speakers is required, it's advisable to protect it with some kind of roof or cover. Waterproof speakers are available but even these should not be totally exposed to the rain for any length of time. Always place speakers either pointing downwards or straight on so the front of the speaker doesn't take the brunt of the rain and fill with water.

Hiring

Sound kits can be bought or hired. Depending on the hire company's policy, it may require that its own staff be present to work the equipment. However, this is rarely the case if the production company has an experienced sound engineer.

Microphones

Some performers may need to use handheld,

stand or radio microphones. Radio microphones are usually attached over the ears or across the hairline and are connected to a transmitter, preferably hidden within the costume. Float or rifle microphones can be used to amplify large groups of performers on stage but aren't so effective outdoors. As well as amplifying the performer's voices, these types of microphones pick up the ambient sounds of cars, aeroplanes, audience noise etc. and should be reserved for indoor use.

Judging the quality of the sound

A sound designer or engineer will always prefer to operate the sound from the same position as the audience in order accurately to gauge its quality. If the sound operator is enclosed within a structure, the operator will ideally want the sides to be removed so that the most accurate version of what the audience is

144

hearing will be heard by him/her. If a particularly unusual space won't allow this, a walkie-talkie can be used, but this is not the perfect solution and only a very experienced sound operator can work in this way. If a performance space is very large, the actors may not be able to hear their cues so a walkie-talkie system could also be used by stage management in this situation. In some productions, a tannoy system is set up backstage to enable the performers to listen for their cues.

Getting permission

In built up areas, permission will need to be sought from the local council's environmental health officer for the legal use of amplified sound. The control of noise (including music from public address systems) is covered by environmental protection legislation, and it is in regard to noise levels that most complaints about an event are made. The legal requirements for amplified sound vary from council to council, and each event is assessed on its merit. Most councils recommend that the company advises local residents of their intentions as a gesture of goodwill. They also stipulate that, in a built-up area, an event using amplification for music or speech must end by eleven o'clock at night. Sound designers can help to contain the sound by pointing the speakers away from residential areas or by choosing specialist speakers that reduce noise levels and direct the sound in a specific direction.

STAGING AND SEATING

The physical dynamics of the site, the type of production and the audience numbers expected will influence the staging and seating arrangements. The arrangement will be partly a practical decision – it's essential the audience sees the action – and partly a creative one. The use of a 'traditional' stage, or raised playing area, and raked seating will inevitably lead to less interaction with the audience. They both create a physical barrier between the performers and the audience. The closer the outdoor setting resembles a traditional indoor theatre, with fixed seating and a proscenium arched stage, the more likely the audience will behave in the manner of an indoor theatre audience. If there is no fixed seating and audience members are free to sit where they choose, then an assessment will need to be made regarding the maximum audience capacity in relation to the site.

Staging possibilities

There are various staging possibilities a company might wish to explore. Although they may replicate some of the techniques used in indoor theatre, some are better suited to an outdoor theatre setting. Here are just some examples:

* Construct a scaffolding structure one storey high or more with the addition of balconies, ladders or bridges.
* Use wheeled carts, platforms or wagons, which can be moved about the space. They can denote different locations or scene changes and can be multi-functional.
* Place items such as furniture, ladders or barrels in such a way that they create different levels within the space or adapt the existing habitat, which might include trees, sand etc. It is not always important that the performers stand on the same 'stage' to communicate.
* Use physical performers such as trapeze artists or rope walkers or adapt simple circus conventions, for example stilt walking.
* Choose a space with a naturally lower area for the action to take place in, for example a quarry or hill. This will allow more playing levels to be added if required.

Two-tiered stage created using scaffolding and 'dressed' with oversized 'washing'. International Festival of the Sea, Portsmouth, 2001.

Placing the audience

The location of audience members in relation to the playing area and their ability to see and hear the show is a company's priority. After all, they are the reason the production is being performed in the first place. It is alarmingly easy for companies to get carried away with the artistic vision and lose sight of what is practical or desirable for an audience. For example, some productions require the audience to stand throughout the piece. This may suit the needs of the company but if the production runs to three hours, is it practical for the audience? Decisions like this are critical as they fundamentally change the dynamics of a piece. Any company should be fully aware before any decisions are finalized how different configurations affect the relationship between the audience and the performers.

Trying out the space

If a company already has a space but isn't sure how to use it, a simple strategy is to try it out. Start by placing an object or person in the space and then walk around looking at it or him/her from different angles. Use more than one person if possible and fill the space with objects that may be used in the final production or bear a close resemblance to them. Engage all the members of the production team and get feedback on the good and bad points of the space. Finally, make sure you consider the audience in relation to the whole space, both acoustically and visually.

Building a stage

As mentioned above, a stage can take many forms (*see* page 145). It could be that the environment has done the job for you or that, with some adaptation, the stage can be created from the surroundings. It can be a huge undertaking to build a stage, so scrutinize the performance to see if one is really necessary. Many outdoor productions use a stage simply because they're copying the conventions of indoor theatre.

Of course, a stage does offer some benefits, such as a raised playing area or a defined playing space, but there are other options. If a raised platform is needed, there are several companies that hire stages, and they can fulfil almost any brief, from raked floor surfaces to bridges and trapdoors.

A popular alternative to hiring a bespoke stage is to use scaffolding and steel deck, which

Bridge constructed over a deep ravine to allow audience members to pass safely, Claremont, 2006. (Photo: Peter Watters)

A 'shipwreck' stage created with steel decking and clad in timber, which makes for a strong stage that is quick to construct, Portsmouth, 2005.

is simple and cost effective. Both allow the set designer more freedom to design the area, as he/she starts with an empty space.

HEALTH AND SAFETY

Risk assessments

A company is required to complete a risk assessment of all areas and give it to the local council's health and safety officials. The community events officer at the council will be able to supply a risk assessment form and other relevant information. A risk assessment demonstrates that the company has taken all the necessary precautionary steps to avoid any risk to public safety. It is a written record of areas where property may be damaged or harm caused to the public, and identifies actions that – as far as is reasonably practical – will reduce or remove these risks. Risk assessments are a legal requirement under the Management of Health and Safety at Work regulations and are restricted to work activities and those affected by them, i.e. employees, visitors etc.

Risk assessments are especially important if the production uses electrical or other forms of power for lighting and sound equipment. If you are using a professional company for any fireworks or incendiary elements, it must produce evidence of its risk assessment, health and safety arrangements and insurance. When planning a large-scale event, always seek professional assistance to ensure all the necessary health and safety measures are in place. The risk assessment must incorporate all safety aspects required for the event e.g. crowd control, evacuation procedures, car parking, toilets and safety barriers. Any structure which is temporary and load bearing must be erected in strict compliance with health and safety regulations. The directive *Five Steps to Risk Assessments* is produced by the Health and Safety Executive and contains recent changes in legislation and advice on effective risk assessment. For more detailed information, always contact the local council, which will advise on risk assessments and health and safety matters in the borough.

First aid

The company must provide a sufficient level of first aid, paramedical or medical facilities as appropriate. To comply with this, consult with the local Ambulance Service, the St John Ambulance or Red Cross voluntary groups, as appropriate. If the event is planned to be large scale, it's generally a good idea to inform the local hospitals, just in case.

Pyrotechnics and fireworks

The use of pyrotechnics and fireworks is becoming increasingly popular in outdoor theatre and can be extremely safe when the guidelines are followed and the proper equipment used. There is a huge range of effects available, and professional companies will advise on the health and safety requirements for each effect. These companies will also supply the necessary staff if an effect requires a licensed operator.

Fire and flame proofing

The use of fire includes anything with an open flame, fireworks and pyrotechnics. Fire extinguishers and buckets of sand should always be positioned in areas of risk. For more information about fire and public events, visit the website, www.fire.gov.uk.

As for flame proofing, the designer or stage manager should be aware of the rules that govern scenery and props and should ensure the production fully complies. In general, if something is carried onto the stage as a prop, it will not have to be flame proofed, whereas anything that is considered a piece of the set should be able to withstand a flame held to it for ten seconds without catching alight or

Paradise Gardens Festival culminated in a huge pyrotechnic and firework display behind In the Doldrums, *Victoria Park, London, 2007.*

continuing to burn after the flame has been removed.

Some materials are inherently flame proof, such as wool, silk, hard woods and metals. Other materials can be bought already flame proofed for use on stage, for example grade one timber, some hessians and gauzes. Ideally, the entire set should be made from flame-proofed fabrics and materials but this isn't always affordable or practical. Quite often items are borrowed, bought new or made from scratch and will therefore require a flame-proof coating. One of the most popular flame-proofing products is called 'Flambar'. It's widely available at theatrical scenic suppliers and can be applied onto scenic elements by brush or spray.

Making the site safe

Many companies concentrate on getting the site free of hazards, whilst forgetting that the entire route into and out of the site will also need to be made safe. Dangerous obstructions have to be moved or cordoned off and signposted. Steep inclines and declines should be adapted with steps or a ramp if the same route is to be used by wheelchair users, and the full route should be well lit if it's to be utilized after dark. The audience capacity will determine the number of entrances and exits needed, and the width of any entrances/exits should be at least 110cm (3ft 6in) to accommodate wheelchair users.

Fencing

Fencing can be used to keep an audience away from potential hazards such as unsafe structures, the lighting and sound equipment, electric cabling and pyrotechnics. Simple wooden or canvas fencing will usually be sufficient for smaller productions, but some companies can supply more robust barriers and fencing if required. Be aware that the fencing surrounding a space will rarely prevent non-ticket holders from standing just the other side of the barrier to watch the action. Fencing works as much to define the space as it does to keep people out.

Site security

If there is any expensive equipment on site, the space will need to be made secure overnight and during the day. Valuable pieces should be stored in lockable units, and hired marquees or cabins can be used to keep safe the costumes and props. Use tarpaulins to protect stage areas or pieces of set when not in use. If the vicinity has a high crime rate (and the budget allows), employ the services of a security firm. Some lighting and sound hire companies provide this service as part of the hire.

Further information

The National Outdoor Events Association has created a handbook called the *Code of Practice for Outdoor Events*, which is an invaluable source of information on all aspects of outdoor theatre. It also contains a list of accredited suppliers.

THE AFTERMATH

To enable a quick and efficient get out, the stage manager should give each member of

Simple interlocking barriers control the flow of audience members coming into the More London venue to watch Scoop Theatre Company's production of Helen of Troy, 2007.

Technical theatre students from the Central School of Speech and Drama dismantling the lighting equipment during a get out at the Minack Theatre. (Photo: Keith Orton)

the cast a specific task. Sound and lighting technicians normally take responsibility for their equipment and make sure that everything is packed securely into flight cases. Wardrobe staff should wash and dry the costumes and pack them ready for travel. They will either go to the next venue, back into storage or be returned to the costume hire company. (Costume hire companies seldom require the costumes to be washed.)

In small or non-professional companies, performers will often take care of their own costumes and help with the get out. Covered areas, tents, staging and seating will need to be dismantled and transported to the next venue, sent back to storage or prepared for collection by the hire company. If a skip has been hired, its collection needs to be organized. Companies should consider the increased traffic at the end of a production and make every effort to minimize any inconvenience to the local community.

151

Repairing the damage

Any damage to the land or buildings in the space must be restored to the satisfaction of the owners. If the event is staged on council-owned property, damage will be repaired by council contractors and the company will be required to repay the total cost. Because of this possible eventuality, most companies take out insurance, particularly if the grounds or buildings are historic and, consequently, costly to repair.

Restoring the space

The grounds will need to be combed for litter and the local council then contacted for information on how to dispose of waste. It's important that the site is returned to its previous function – if it had one – and left in the state it was in. Your company may not be the only production wishing to use the space and failure to leave the site in good order jeopardizes its use in the future.

Leaving the site

Companies have different ways of leaving the space once the production has finished. This largely depends on the emotional attachment to the space and whether it was site specific. Some companies have a ritual burning of design elements to mark the end of a production – or some kind of ending ceremony – whereas others leave with as little fuss as possible.

Feedback

It is generally good practice for companies to do some sort of post-analysis of the production, and many companies give out questionnaires inviting feedback. It is important that companies review all areas of the technical and artistic work in order to develop the areas that worked well and improve the areas that weren't so successful.

10 PERFORMANCE, PERFORMERS AND REHEARSALS

APPROACHING THE CONTENT

As discussed in Chapter 2, there are several techniques a creative team can use when deciding on the content for a production (*see* page 25). The most common techniques are:

* Using an existing script
* Adapting an existing script
* Exploring a new play written for the company
* Devising a show, with or without a playwright
* A mixture of the above.

How a company approaches the work will depend on the type of show it wants to create or the ethos it works by. Theatre companies don't always approach new productions in the same way. Some are inspired by a location, a story or a text. Other companies may have been commissioned to create new work for which the theme has already been decided, or have received funding to work within a community. There are companies that have adopted one approach, such as working from devised rehearsals, and only ever work in this way. But there's no right or wrong approach to creating a show outdoors. Just bear in mind

that the space should always be considered first before the approach is decided upon.

AUDITIONS

Professional performers

Outdoor theatre often requires a range of skills and abilities from the performers. They have to work with numerous distractions, such as bad weather and ambient noise, so a director should try and cast performers who either have previous experience of performing outdoors or the skills to adapt to an outdoor setting. Most directors will try to cast performers possessing good movement and verbal skills. It's important to make the performers aware of the reality of working outdoors. Along with bright sunshine and balmy summer evenings, it can also be wet, uncomfortable and hard work, especially for the voice. If the show is touring, the performers may well be expected to help with the get in and get out. If this is so, make sure they are aware of what is required from them so that problems will be avoided later in the tour.

It's not always necessary to cast performers who have training in formal acting. The production may require skills from other back-

153

London Bubble Theatre Company's performance of **The Dong with the Luminous Nose,** *2007. (Photo: John Stanley-Clamp)*

grounds, such as dance, circus or mime. London Bubble Theatre Company has a novel approach to the audition process. It asks each actor to come to the audition with a story to tell – and sometimes elements of the story are included in or inform the theme of the produc- tion. Finally, make sure performers are fully scrutinized for the role they are expected to play. If they state that they have certain skills or abilities, ask them to prove it. It will save a lot of time and disappointment if this turns out not to be the case.

Community plays or amateur productions

Community plays usually have an all-inclusive casting policy so remember that most people auditioning for a role will have little or no previous acting experience. Make sure auditions are relaxed and informal. Professional performers are at an audition because they want the job and expect to be rigorously examined. Amateur performers are there on a voluntary basis and should be treated completely differently. Group exercises and games are an excellent way of getting people relaxed and also of finding out what skills they may have to offer. It's a good idea to choose people not just for their talent but also for their willingness to try out new ideas. Their ability to be inventive and come up with solutions will make the production a much better one.

'To find again a lost technique – the style of playing highly alliterate verse, designed for public speaking in public spaces. It is verse energetic enough to surmount the noise of passers by and tough enough, with its defining consonants, never to die on the wind; a truly public speech.'

(Sir Peter Hall, talking about the mystery plays performed at the National Theatre in 1985)

Mimbre Company's show, The Bridge, *performed outside the National Theatre on London's Southbank as part of its Watch This Space season, 2007. The performers communicated only in Swedish and Italian, but used acrobatics, theatre techniques and dance to tell their story and create imagery. (Photo: Stuart Wyatt)*

155

TECHNIQUES FOR PERFORMANCE

Once the performers have been cast, the rehearsals or devising process will begin. The majority of indoor theatre shows rely on the spoken word to tell the story. Since an outdoor theatre production has to compete with the scale, noise and diversions of an outdoor setting, the director may want to employ other techniques, as well as the spoken word, to portray the action. It is worth pointing out that performers often do not speak loud enough in outdoor theatre shows and need to be reminded to project their voice. The volume they are accustomed to working at may not be loud enough, especially in a large production with a larger audience.

Communicating to the audience

The acting styles, and consequently the directing techniques, will obviously change depending on the size of the audience. Generally speaking, free shows will attract larger crowds than paying performances and the duration of the run will also have an impact on audience numbers. A free event for one night will create a much bigger audience than an event spread over two weeks. More intimate shows that cater for smaller audiences will be able to use subtle devices, whereas larger productions will have to rely on much broader techniques.

Puppet approaching from the distance, looming over the brow of a hill in Full House Theatre Company's production of **Robin Hood.** *(Photo: Keith Orton)*

'Shadowy figure' masks worn on various parts of the head, especially on the crown, to create less human characters and to enable the mask to be seen by audience members high up in the raked seating at the Minack Theatre, Cornwall. A **Time Machine,** *designed by Nina Ayres and students from the Central School of Speech and Drama, 2005. (Photo: Keith Orton)*

Supporting the narrative

There are techniques other than words that can be used to tell or support the narrative.

Puppetry

One of the advantages of outdoor theatre is that it offers enormous scope for puppets to be used on practically any scale. Small puppets can be used either en masse or specifically where applicable. Large puppets can also be accommodated if the space allows.

Masks

A full face mask works well when combined with large gestures, but it can be difficult to hear a performer wearing a full mask. Half masks allow a performer to speak much more clearly. Masks can also be worn on different parts of the head to work from the back or top or to create more than one character.

Rapid transformations

One of the best-known transformation techniques is found in the Japanese mask theatre of Kabuki. It uses expressive masks to distinguish between the characters and allows the performers instantly to change roles. But various other costumes and props

Goat masks worn on the back of the head by members of the chorus during a production of The Bacchae *by Thiasos Theatre Company, 2004. Designed by Abdel'kader Farrah.*
(Photo: Yana Zarifi)

can be used to transform characters – wigs, hats, glasses and body padding are all excellent devices. A character's transformation doesn't have to be done away from the stage. The audience will forgive – and in most cases delight in – the transformation as long as this device is continued throughout the piece.

Physical theatre

Using large or exaggerated movements helps the audience to identify the characters. Physical theatre is one of the most effective performance techniques in an outdoor setting and is often performed in conjunction with masks. The Italian theatre tradition of *commedia dell'arte* has influenced many physical theatre movements and theatrical styles throughout the centuries. The comic style, coupled with acrobatic and gestured movements, dispenses with any subtleties and leaves little room for misinterpretation.

'*Commedia dell'arte* evolved essentially as an outdoor style with big gestures, lots of physicality, loud and in your face, and *lazzi, burli* and what we call 'knots' require space. It's very hard to adapt to a village hall where sometimes we have to retreat if it rains.'

(Pete Talbot, artistic director,
The Rude Mechanical Theatre Company)

Scale and height

Outdoor theatre is the perfect space to play with scale and height. A company can make elements oversized or may choose to scale them down. Whether reducing or enlarging, the techniques can be used for a variety of dramatic effects; to give something extra significance, to convey humour or ridicule, to interact with the performers or the audience – the list is endless. Bear in mind that simply because you can dramatically increase, or decrease, the scale of an element, it doesn't automatically follow you should. For example, the use of stilts can act as a metaphor regarding a character's elevated status. But if this device is employed without a context, the effect will be lost so be selective in your choices.

Music

Live music can be particularly atmospheric outdoors, and can be played either off stage or on stage by the performers or musicians. Even

The Rude Mechanical Theatre Company's production of Five Get Famous, 2007, *showing the use of large, exaggerated gestures by the performers.* (Photo: John Stanley-Clamp)

Beachcomber *by Boilerhouse in collaboration with the Dutch company De Waterlanders.*
A site-specific piece of outdoor theatre created at Tershchelling as part of the Oerol Festival,
2007. Because of the outsized table, performers had to stand on chairs in order to reach
the tabletop. (Photo: Simon Meadows)

if the performers do not play traditional instruments, there are still many ways they can create music. Using props or the set to make banging noises or to create a beat is always effective, for example when accompanying a scene involving a fight. Performers might play whistles, blow horns or use non-musical instruments to announce the change of a scene, introduce a character or simply to accompany the music.

Oil drums, pyrotechnics and fireworks
Larger outdoor theatre events have become synonymous with the use of fire in one form or another. Fire invariably adds drama to a scene and often creates a visually stunning spectacle. Smaller outdoor theatre shows can employ these devices in simpler, low-scale ways by using flaming torches, burning oil drums or lanterns. Pyrotechnics and fireworks should only be used if they support the narrative, for example to add drama to an explosion, and should not be relied upon to add a 'glamorous' finish to the end of an evening.

Dance
Dance can help to coordinate the performers both rhythmically and aesthetically. This can range from simple choreographed steps that look like natural movements to large dance pieces involving the whole cast.

A simple pyrotechnic device was used to show the 'time machine' exploding. Designed by Nina Ayres in conjunction with students from the Central School of Speech and Drama. Minack Theatre, 2005. (Photo: Keith Orton)

Repetition

Audience members' attention is more likely to wander in an outdoor environment, but there may be crucial moments when they need to pay attention. A simple technique to focus an audience is repetition. Repetition can take the form of dialogue, movement, music, props or set and, in some cases, the space will allow an echo effect.

Setting

Directors should always be aware of the impact deriving from the space the perform-ance inhabits. Techniques and conventions can be explored that don't exist in conven-tional indoor theatres. The setting is more than a stage, it's a space to be fully explored. Here is just one example that neatly demon-strates this: a character who dies might walk off into the distance until he/she is lost over the horizon or amongst the trees. It's simple, effective and inhabits the whole space rather than just the playing area.

Biuro Podróży

An example of a company that uses many of

Thiasos Theatre Company's production of The Persians *takes full advantage of the enormous steps, which became part of the set for the touring production in Oxford, 2006.*

the above techniques is a Polish theatre company called Biuro Podróży. They created a large-scale outdoor production, entitled *Who is that Bloodied Man?*, which was a reworking of *Macbeth*. The company reduced Shakespeare's text to the most minimal use of words and relied on physical theatre to tell the story.

The show successfully created potent symbols and metaphors to help the audience follow the story: Macbeth's victims were represented by felled tree trunks, Lady Macbeth's murderous influence was represented by a woman eating an apple and tempting her lover with it, and Macbeth's bloody rise and fall were told

'The challenge for theatre makers at this point, especially when working with large audiences is this: how do you create a theatre experience that is a real genuine emotional and intellectual engagement, so that it's not just eye candy? Got to have that, some sort of visual impact but at the same time where do you get that intellectual content from.'

(Paul Pinson, artistic director, Boilerhouse)

through a mix combining pyrotechnics and motorbikes. The conscious choice to tell the story visually rather than textually enabled the company to tour Europe without the need to alter the language of the show.

REHEARSALS AND EXPLORATION OF THE SITE

It's very unlikely that a company will use the actual space for rehearsals, although it's obviously preferable to do so. Even if the space is available, rehearsals may not be practical because of, for example, the weather, lack of on-site facilities or access. Initially, a company might use the space for workshops if it is embarking on a piece of site-specific theatre, but it's also crucial that the company and cast experience the specific site in which they will be performing.

Utilizing the space at the Minack Theatre in Cornwall during a production by Central School of Speech and Drama. (Photo: Keith Orton)

163

The Princess, the Palace and the Ice Cold Bath *exploits the space by having 'gardeners' in the opening scene far in the distance on the other side of the lake. Claremont, Surrey, 2006.*

Site-specific exploration

There are several methods that can be employed to help the company fully explore the potential of the space it will be performing in:

* Explore the site from a distance as well as close up and write a list of initial responses or ideas. The list should include how the site feels as well as looks, making particular reference to anything that the space is reminiscent of. These findings can be a good starting point for the artistic vision of the production.

* Place objects or people – with or without masks on – in the space and view them from every conceivable angle. This will roughly determine what looks 'right' and which objects or people look incongruous. It might also help to create stories as to why this might be the case.

* Research and share the history of the space, whether real or mythological. Any findings may help to push the production into new areas or significantly change the themes and narrative of the piece.

'We often find an intriguing, resonant site ...
We actively seek them ...
We don't always make a new work with a new site ...
Once a site has been found, if we feel that there is a richness and a potential there that would add to the meaning of the story, we would seek to recreate an existing work for that place and with the people of that place. The work folds in and around itself, gaining in richness and resonance.
It is the same for all of our work ... nothing gets wasted.'

(WildWorks' philosophy statements)

The rehearsal space

Whether rehearsing for a site-specific, touring or static piece of theatre, the venue chosen for rehearsals should closely resemble the size of the site(s). Start by marking the floor to show the configuration of the playing area, with exits and entrances clearly identified. The farthest reaches of an audience should also be marked and the elevation of an audience should be indicated to make the performers aware of their eye-line.

Directors should always watch rehearsals from the audience's perspective. It's a good idea to move around the space to help the performers relate to the whole audience, not just one section. If the audience will be on raked seating, rig a scaffold structure so the director can view and direct the action from the position of the audience. When rehearsing in a confined space, it's easy to forget the potential of space above the action and off in to the distance. Going outdoors, even if it's not the playing area, can be a brilliant way to open up ideas and remind yourself what all that space feels like in times of creative stagnation.

If the show is to tour to a variety of different sites, a defined playing area should be chosen for rehearsals. This will then create a playing template that can be extended or reduced depending on the size of the venue.

Making the performers comfortable

It's important for performers to start working with the set, props, puppets, masks and any elaborate costumes as soon as possible. The stage manager should provide substitute items to rehearse with until the finished ones are ready. Using substitutes is useful, but performers can become so comfortable with 'stand-in' models that they then encounter problems when the real objects arrive.

When staging a community play, cast members need to feel comfortable with their environment, costumes and props. Consequently, community cast members should have as much rehearsal time as possible with the more intricate pieces of set or props. Of course this isn't always possible and in some cases the stage manager will struggle to find alternatives. But as a general rule, props and sets should be rehearsed with as early as possible. Also, by doing so, previously unexplored possibilities on how to use the items may open up.

Rehearsing masks and puppets

A good way of rehearsing with masks and puppets is to do so in front of a mirror (dance studios are ideal for this). This will enable performers to see how effectively they're moving the puppet and to make sure they position the correct eye-line. No amount of instructions from a director can compensate for the effect of seeing it first hand. The same technique can also be used for mask work. If there is more than one masked performer on stage, it is invaluable that everyone rehearses in front of a mirror. This helps each performer to see what the others are doing and how they should be working as a group. If a mirrored

Blobby puppets designed by Nina Ayres.

Puppets with extendable legs being used in the performance of A Time Machine, *Central School of Speech and Drama, at the Minack Theatre, Cornwall, 2005.*

studio isn't available or if the puppets are too big to be rehearsed indoors, then a good alternative is to video the performer manipulating the puppet. They will then have a better idea of how their actions and movements look.

Working together

There are many games and exercises that theatre directors use in rehearsal to help performers work as a group. It is especially important that performers trust their colleagues in an outdoor production, as there is a risk of the unexpected happening. Jon Oram, artistic director of Claque Theatre Company, includes

a description of 'Theatre games' on the Company's website which outlines many of these exercises.

THE PERFORMANCE

Performers should always do vocal and physical warm-ups before the show to ensure they don't lose their voice or suffer an injury. This is especially important in outdoor venues as the colder temperatures considerably increase the risk of straining parts of the body that haven't been warmed up properly. The warm-up can be done individually or as a group and will

> 'Break down theatrical conventions, stage events in a way that includes the audience.'
>
> (Richard Schechner, in his essay *Six Axioms of Environmental Theatre*)

often involve vocal exercises, repeating text or songs from the production or playing a verbal/physical game.

The lack of traditional stage amenities in outdoor theatre can be demanding for performers. Often, there are neither wings nor dressing room available to relax in when they are off stage. Consequently, outdoor productions can be physically exhausting because performers may be required to be on stage for all, or most, of the piece.

Involving the audience

An enormous amount of humour can be had from interacting with the audience. All sorts of techniques can be used to involve audience members in the action: asking them to hold real or imagined objects, serving them drinks or canapés or indeed having part of their picnic 'crashed' by an actor. During its show *Metamorphosis*, the London Bubble Theatre Company even gave out pieces of lighting gel

A performer from The Rude Mechanical Theatre Company mingling with the audience at its reworked version of A Midsummer Night's Dream. *(Photo: John Stanley-Clamp)*

to shade the audience's eyes from the sun. The humour derived from the fact that the audience was warned of the brightness of 'the sun', which turned out to be a simple low-wattage lantern.

The unexpected

Performing in an open, sometimes public, space inevitably throws up the unexpected. However thorough a company has been in assessing risks, things can still go wrong. It will often be the responsibility of the performers immediately to resolve the problem. An experienced performer will embrace a situation that's gone wrong and turn it around to his/her advantage. Indeed, such a moment can often be the highlight of the production.

For example, if the lights go out on stage – an event that is all too common in outdoor theatre – the performer(s) can either choose to stand around and wait until the problem is fixed or see the funny side and share a joke with the audience until the lights are back on or until the stage manager makes an announcement.

Keeping the audience's attention

There will always be something to distract the audience outdoors and performers will need to work hard in an outdoor setting to keep its attention focused. Performers will need instinctively to know when to break the flow of the piece in order to let the distraction pass.

'Audience members of outdoor shows always seem to be on the side of the performer, they appear to appreciate the willingness of the actors to present a show in a potentially hostile environment and they want it to work. The audience members love to feel that they are witnessing something unique and sharing something special with each other and the cast. The best parts of a show or, at least, the parts that the audience fondly remembers can be the moments when something doesn't work, when a performer forgets an action or fails an attempt at doing something. An outdoor audience relishes these moments only if the response to these failings by a performer is taken light heartedly and almost with a wink towards the audience as a way of reiterating the 'we're in this together' vibe.'

(Sonia Ritter, artistic director, Lions part Theatre Company)

Equally, it's important they judge when to continue during a disturbance and adjust their performance accordingly. It's always a good idea for the performer to acknowledge the distraction in character, even if he/she decides to continue through it. Possible reactions can range from the performer joining the audience and watching the disturbance together to leaving the playing area and becoming directly involved in the distraction.

11 Now and the Future

Pioneering companies

An increasing number of theatre-goers are becoming disillusioned with the indoor format of the traditional proscenium arch. This is a trend that has been evolving since the 1960s, when many theatre practitioners began to break away from the proscenium mould and offered alternative staging configurations. The desire to re-establish theatre as a popular and immediate work of art, one that speaks directly to the people, was brought about by radical theatre groups during the 1970s and 1980s. It's from this time that much of our modern outdoor theatre originates.

Companies that formed decades ago are still some of the most exciting companies producing outdoor theatre today. With a background in anarchic theatre, they have been at the forefront in pushing the boundaries of what is acceptable in theatrical terms and what structures can be used to tell the story. Many companies tend to work in alternative venues, either indoors or outdoors, and want the freedom to explore the potential of theatrical performance as a whole, without being typecast into a defined genre.

Companies such as Emergency Exit, IOU, Pentabus, Bread and Puppet, People Show and Dodgy Clutch are just some of the companies still producing challenging work and striving to make theatre accessible to a wider section of society.

The People Show

The People Show began in 1966 and is generally considered to have been the first experimental theatre group in the UK. They began by giving small performances in the basement of a bookshop in central London, effectively helping to redefine the laws by which theatre was governed at the time. They quickly amassed a cult following, but due to the unscripted and experimental nature of their work, the company stayed beyond the realms of mainstream theatre circles. They are a unique company in that their shows are always devised by one or more multi-disciplinary artists. These artists make up a core team within the company, negating the need for outside writers or directors.

Dodgy Clutch

Dodgy Clutch Theatre Company was formed in 1982. Since then it has worked with a growing number of freelance artists who share its belief that theatre is an enriching experience and should be accessible to everyone. It works collaboratively to produce new work in a popular form of visual theatre, combining the different theatrical elements of music, dance, performance, mime and puppetry. In the past twenty years, Dodgy Clutch has cultivated site-specific, large-scale events in non-traditional venues, with a particular interest in the north east of England. One of its company aims is to 'enhance the quality, standards and value of the work and therefore make it more rewarding to its expanding audiences.'

Pageant segment of Bread and Puppet Theatre's Victory Over Everything *circus and pageant,* **2006.** *(Photo: Jack Sumberg)*

Pentabus

Pentabus was founded in 1974 to stage new writing in the five counties of the Midlands. Today, it tours to small- and middle-scale venues throughout the country. Its production entitled *Silent Engine* won an Edinburgh Fringe First award in 2002 and an Arts Council of England New Writing Award in 2003. The Company has a strong reputation for large-scale outdoor productions, such as its show *Precious Bane*, which harnessed all the essential elements: the sun, earth, fire, water – and even a real horse. It also operates a writer's development programme and runs extensive education projects throughout the year.

These and many other companies are still striving to break down the rules and restrictions that indoor theatre imposes on outdoor productions. They wish to recapture an audience that has been lost to the art form and are prepared to take theatre directly to those people and share it with them. Even companies with a strong reputation for their indoor theatre work have begun to explore the outdoor arena and the possibilities it brings. The Birmingham Repertory Theatre created a

'This to me, was complete outdoor theatre. Not television, not film but a live event, reminding me of the old medieval mummer carts, which used to tour villages long ago – the very origins of taking theatre to the community – which in those days delivered news and parables not through your door but in the town square, in your face.

This was all complemented and married to the Welford Park grounds, with the audience sitting on rugs and camp-chairs in an informal structure. It was ultimately capped by a superb flock of thirty geese – on cue, twice wheeling over Welford Park towards the south and then changing its mind and returning as dusk fell.'

(Euan Smith, journalist, on *Precious Bane*)

show called *Box* in 2006, in which forty-three audience members, seated on a narrow boat, watched the action unfold along six miles of waterway towpaths. Its intention was to provide an event that both embraced Birmingham's canal heritage and also gave non-professional performers from the local community the opportunity to take part.

TEACHING OUTDOOR THEATRE

More and more companies are attracted to an explorative type of theatre, and it's now taught as part of many theatre and performance degree courses. Schools and colleges, such as the Central School of Speech and Drama and East 15, are now providing courses with

Revellers and performers alike take part in the ancient celebration of the Green Man in Hastings. (Photo: Simon Costin)

The Lions part Theatre Company performing mummers' play **October Plenty** *on London's Southbank. (Photo: Robert Thomson)*

strong elements of community theatre and projects directly based on site-specific work. This growing interest should produce more practitioners and performers and continue the growth of outdoor theatre.

In addition to schools and colleges, many established theatre companies are looking further than mere performances as a way to generate extra income and pass their experience on to a new generation. The People Show is a good example of a company who do this. They rent their studio space to other companies when not in use and have a 'New Work Clinic', which seeks to offer advice to emerging companies in need of an expert eye. They also extend their artistic programme by working with schools, colleges and community organizations, as well as offering lectures, workshops and residencies. Likewise Pentabus operates a writer's development programme and runs extensive education projects throughout the year. The number of courses and workshops on offer represents the growing interest in the subject.

173

'Thousands of people who wouldn't normally step inside a theatre are attracted to these outdoor productions.'

(Lynn Gardner, *The Guardian*,
June 23, 2004)

RENEWAL OF ANCIENT TRADITIONS

In addition to new works, there has been a renewed interest in Britain's ancient forms of outdoor theatre, which all but died out when theatre moved indoors at the start of the twentieth century. Seasonal celebrations, such as May Day and Jack in the Green, are enjoying a revival, as are festivals concerning local food and drink, for example harvest celebrations. It could be that, as we're becoming more aware of the environment, we want to return to and celebrate, as a society, more traditional ways of living.

Mummers' plays today

Although most mummers' plays had almost died out by the beginning of the twentieth century, a few continued to be performed in villages around the UK. Today many modern theatre companies have rediscovered the mummers' tradition, and some town councils actively encourage companies to perform at festivals and local celebrations. Bampton Mummers is one of a handful of companies that traces its history back to the nineteenth century. Abingdon Mummers holds a 'town tour' before Christmas, followed by a 'world tour' of nearby villages. The Traditional Drama Research group lists performances around the country on its website.

Mystery plays today

Towns and cities that were originally associated with mystery plays began to renew their interest in them in the 1950s and 1960s. People began to research their history and revive various pageants in a form as true as possible to the original productions. There are now more and more mystery plays performed every year. A good example is the modern Guilds of York, whose first formal association with a 'waggon' production was in 1998. The Guilds' involvement came about as a result of artistic director June Oakshot, who believed that, in order for the mystery plays to be produced accurately, local guilds should be an integral part of the production. In 2002, the Guilds took charge of the production, and, in 2006, twelve 'waggons' rolled through the streets with support from the City Council and the Early Music Festival. The company of, mostly, volunteers, local amateur dramatics companies and guilds' people took the fundamental elements of the mystery plays and successfully adapted them for a modern audience

'We wish to bring some lost sense of the joy and loveliness of the passing seasons and our rich heritage that is inspired by them. This may be relevant in the unbalanced high-tech, stressed urban society of today in so far as it may lifts spirits, create a sense of well-being and open up people's imagination.

Reclaiming public spaces for entertainment is one of the best things to have happened in the last twenty years despite the crippling and stifling effect of current 'bureaucratized' health and safety fears. I think it is very popular indeed. Witness the 'pedestrianization' of Trafalgar Square – now a place of public entertainment, to the resurgence of the village fête.'

(Sonia Ritter, artistic director,
Lions part Theatre Company)

One of the pageant wagons in the City of York as part of its re-enactment of The York
Mystery Plays *by York Festival Trust, 2002. (Photo: York Festival Trust)*

in a modern setting. Other towns famous for their mystery plays include Chester and Wakefield, where the plays, involving hundreds of local people in the production, both on and off stage, are performed every four years.

SHAKESPEARE AND THE CLASSICS

There has been a steady rise in the number of companies, both professional and amateur, that stage Shakespeare's plays and other classics outdoors. This type of production comprises the largest sector of outdoor theatre and is almost certain of attracting an audience. The companies involved invariably choose National Trust sites or areas of historic significance and natural beauty. However, it would be fair to say that their contribution to the art of outdoor theatre as a whole is rather insignificant. Shakespeare – and other early forms of outdoor theatre – did not pay homage to the open space: they simply had no choice but to play outdoors. It seems incongruous then, that many productions feel the need to 'perform' as Shakespeare did. There are now countless well-equipped venues, which are designed to maximize the acoustics, provide seating with a clear view and keep an audience protected from the weather. With this in mind, I must reiterate the point that outdoor theatre should strive to provide an experience beyond what can be achieved indoors.

So many productions attempt to replicate the configuration of an indoor venue and completely ignore how the production might interact with the space. Of course, there are companies that do excellent work with classic texts and reinvent the work for an outdoor space. It's not the fault of the text, but more often the fault of the creative vision. In conclusion, companies using classic texts need to make sure that they are creating a piece of outdoor theatre and not just taking a piece of indoor theatre and staging it outdoors. Not only does this waste the potential of outdoor theatre, but it can also be counterproductive for the performers and audience alike.

CORPORATE EVENTS AND OUTDOOR THEATRE

Corporations have begun to employ outdoor theatre companies to entertain their customers or staff at corporate events. Theatre companies offering circus skills, puppetry, acrobatic or walkabout techniques are in particular demand. Spectacular performances involving sound, light and pyrotechnics are increasingly fashionable, and the budgets for these shows are growing each year. And it's not just big corporate events that use outdoor theatre techniques. Even office parties and opening ceremonies are utilizing the skills of theatre companies.

It's obviously economically rewarding for theatre companies to accept this type of employment. It's also pleasing that more people are exposed to the techniques of outdoor theatre. But there is some cause for concern. By fulfilling clients' expectations for the production to be a spectacle, companies may start to produce a formularized 'type' of outdoor production. Worse, the formula used would owe more to spectacle than narrative, and the concern would be that the 'spectacle' would seep into the creative work. If companies believe that an outdoor production has to involve some sort of spectacular element to be successful, it would be severely detrimental to the piece and the art form as a whole. So far, this has mostly been avoided, but it will be interesting to see if outdoor theatre companies continue to follow their artistic beliefs in new and challenging work.

The magnificent De La Warr Pavilion, Bexhill, utilizing their outdoor area wonderfully during their 'Jour de Fête'. (Photo: Paul Hewitt)

COMMISSIONS AND FESTIVALS

Commissions

Many companies are now being commissioned to produce shows for specific events or festivals. They can be commissioned for a variety of reasons: as part of an established outdoor or street theatre festival, as part of a regeneration project or to mark a historic date. Commissioned theatre pieces are often free to the public and an excellent way of bringing theatre to people who wouldn't normally see it. Companies with an established reputation for outdoor theatre work are sometimes fortunate enough to have entire projects funded through commission.

A good example of this is Emergency Exit Arts, founded in 1980 and now one of the UK's largest street arts companies. They have twenty-eight years of experience in devising and producing performances and community-

> 'There seem to be more companies getting on the bandwagon and doing outdoor theatre. I think they think with global warming there's going to be more demand and a quick buck can be made. Personally I think the weather is going to get more difficult and erratic, so they may be in for a surprise.'
>
> (Pete Talbot,
> The Rude Mechanical Theatre Company)

Emergency Exit Arts' show **Arena: the Perfect Circle,** *being performed in* **Bournemouth.** *(Photo: Nick Cattermole)*

based arts projects, both large and small scale. For example, the company was commissioned by Nottingham City Council in March 2007 to create a huge extravaganza celebrating the opening of the new Market Square in the cen-tre of the city. On the other hand, commissions, in association with their 'in-house' shows *Runga Rung* and *Arena* see them engage local artists, residents and visitors in an out-reach programme of workshops and projects associated with the show and incorporating local influences and histories. The accumulated work then becomes part of a parade that precedes the show or becomes a part of the show itself. Emergency Exit Arts is a good example of a company that has embraced all kinds of different theatre techniques and is very flexible about the work it can offer, thus maximizing its employment potential. Some of the techniques offered include community celebrations, music, outdoor shows, mechanical sculptures, vehicles and installations, education and training, fireworks, site-specific and, of course, events, festivals and commissions.

'The shows have been devised with a fluidity that enables the outreach, whatever that may be, to be incorporated. But the storyline, action and all the technical ingenuity is very much set. What it does, however, is engage the local community a lot more than just giving them some brief entertainment – they are part of a large outdoor spectacular and take a much longer-lasting experience away with them.'

(Ben Raine, Production Manager, Emergency Exit Arts)

Emergency Exit Arts' show **Runga Rung** *being performed in Craven Arms.*
(Photo: Sabine Hutchinson)

Walk the Plank is another company with a reputation for large-scale theatre work: a creative force of artists, theatre-makers and event engineers – specialists in weaving together performers, visual images, fire, fireworks and music to create outdoor performance and specially-commissioned events. Walk the Plank have been creating high quality and innovative work for the past fifteen years, in the UK and internationally.

Commissions from festivals, art centres and councils are vital for the future development of British outdoor theatre. They are the life-blood of new work, and outdoor theatre needs their support to continue offering audiences new and exciting work.

'Working outdoors allows us to make theatre which engages different audiences in ways which they find exciting and unexpected and which allows us to respond to the site. The locations, the scale (and weather) sometimes shape the story, and the images can create a resonance with the audience that reaches backwards and forwards... to what's gone before and into the future.

(Liz Pugh, Producer of Walk the Plank)

The Emperor and the Tiger – *a collaboration between Walk the Plank and the carnival arts company Kinetica.* (Photo: Dave Sinclair)

> 'The media don't take outdoor work seriously ... they tend to write about the weather and the British 'Dunkirk spirit'. Outdoor work requires a different aesthetic – direct, engaging, clear story telling. Thus it can pull together broad audiences but is unlikely to tickle the fancy of those whose palates are attuned to the Royal Court.'
>
> (Jonathan Petherbridge, artistic director, London Bubble Theatre Company)

Festivals

Festivals of outdoor and street theatre have been gaining in popularity and number since the 1960s. One of the country's leading outdoor festivals is the Winchester Hat Fair. What began as a small street theatre festival in the 1960s now includes community projects, a children's procession, international large-scale work and a variety of commissioned work. To be included in the festival, Hat Fair has only one rule – 'excellence in outdoor and site-specific work'. The event is free, and contribution is based on a 'pay what you can' policy. The UK now plays host to hundreds of similar festivals in many towns and cities. Some of the leading outdoor festivals and their websites are:

* Winchester Hat Fair – www.hatfair.co.uk
* X.trax in Manchester – www.xtrax.org.uk
* Streets of Brighton – www.zapuk.com
* Greenwich and Docklands International Festival in London – www.festival.org
* The Stockton International Riverside Festival – www.sirf.co.uk

There are also renowned international festivals of outdoor theatre, including Fira del Tarrega in Spain, Oerol and Tuig in Holland and the Malta Festival in Poland.

MEDIA INTEREST

For some reason, outdoor theatre doesn't receive the same level of press coverage as other types of theatre. There are mixed feelings among theatre practitioners as to whether this is good or bad. It is argued that freedom from the criticism of newspapers and television leaves companies room for artistic experimentation. Conversely, it's also argued that outdoor theatre needs to be properly critiqued in order to maintain high standards and prevent the form from generating mediocre work.

In 2004, a journalist from a British newspaper wrote an entire article about Improbable Theatre Company's outdoor theatre show *Sticky*. The editor of the newspaper refused to print the article on the basis that the paper didn't cover 'circus'. What made this strange was the fact that all of Improbable Theatre's indoor shows had received full press coverage. Fortunately, the journalist had the article printed with another newspaper, but this tale does underline the negative media attitude to outdoor theatre work.

Despite these setbacks, there is evidence in the growing number of reviews that awareness of outdoor theatre in the media is changing. One of the few publications to consistently review outdoor productions is *Total Theatre Magazine*, which specializes in bringing together all areas of the visual and physical performance sector.

> 'We learned that when you can't persuade theatre critics to write a review, then you should invite the crime, war or sports reporters.'
>
> (John Fox, from his book *Eyes on Stalks*, Welfare State International)

Scottish performance company Boilerhouse's co-production with French theatre company Metalvoice premiered at BIG in Falkirk, Scotland's National Street Arts Festival, in May 2005. The production, entitled 3600″, explored perceptions of time through a mix of video and performance. (Photo: Boilerhouse)

TECHNOLOGY

Outdoor theatre shows are consistently taking advantage of developments in technology, which makes the possibilities for outdoor theatre ever more interesting. Outdoor lighting and sound are becoming more adept at dealing with focused sound and light, and there's now more scope for creating outdoor special effects. Pyrotechnics and fireworks can be better controlled and with greater accuracy than before. One of the genuine technological advancements in outdoor theatre is the use of video projections. These projections were originally used for outdoor cinemas, but some companies have begun to employ them in their productions. Boilerhouse Theatre Company has always used video projection in its outdoor shows to help create the narrative. Artistic director Paul Pinson, whose background is in film, maintains that rather than being a technological intrusion or using technology for its own sake, the projection becomes a character within the piece.

HEALTH AND SAFETY

The health and safety agenda is an issue that is constantly bemoaned by all outdoor theatre practitioners as it becomes ever more stringent and, effectively, stifles creativity. With the growing list of health and safety requirements, it does appear that staging an outdoor theatre show can be more trouble than it's worth. Local councils scrutinize every single element, and the list of objections on the grounds of health and safety, public nuisance, noise pollution and disturbance of peace can deter even the most seasoned outdoor company.

The theatre company Welfare State International disbanded in 2006, after thirty-nine years of large-scale, site-specific outdoor theatre. Its artistic director, John Fox, said the final straw was when he was asked to apply for a 'Hot work' permit to light a bonfire in a field. However, John Fox and Sue Gill continue to work with their new company Dead Good Guides, which picks up where Welfare State International left off in the area between theatre and ritual.

It isn't all doom and gloom. There is still the potential to produce new and invigorating work that's artistically satisfying for both the company and the audience. The fact remains that outdoor theatre reaches an audience that

'All our goals of the 1960s: access, disability awareness, multigenerational and multicultural participation, have been established; but now such agendas come before the art.'

(John Fox from an interview with editors@arts professional.co.uk)

indoor theatre seldom does and, even with increased bureaucracy, companies are continuing to produce work that pushes the art further. Not only are outdoor theatre productions growing year by year, but, more encouragingly, audience members are growing with them.

THE LEGACY

Outdoor theatre, unlike any other type of theatre, has the capacity to make a real impact within the community. At the very least it

The Dancing Sky *at Greenwich and Docklands International Festival 2006 included the use of video projection. (Photo: Alastair Muir)*

Welfare State International's final show, **Longline – The Carnival Opera.** *(Photo: Ged Murray)*

'Participation seems appropriate, not only within the context of a community play, but in a modern culture where community itself is in some sense breaking down. The plays re-introduce methods that are lying dormant. In society in general and in entertainment in particular, the movement is towards the self-contained, electronically processed unresponsive systems – closed systems on which the individual can have little effect. Orthodox theatre is much more open than television or film but the community play strives for greater openness. Promenade theatres' attempts at audience participation opens the system, making feedback not only possible but delightful.'

(Jon Oram, Claque Theatre Company)

offers an alternative and more accessible form of entertainment to people who may not normally go to the theatre. In the case of community plays, it can offer a new sense of ownership of the area. Outdoor theatre is now attracting more serious practitioners, who believe in the need to take theatre directly to the community. There is also a renewed interest in the environment and the impact we're having on it. There is a real opportunity to take the historical elements of outdoor theatre – the Mummers, Harvest Festivals, etc. – and combine them with new theatre techniques. As we look back and take inspiration from the past, we should remember that outdoor theatre, as an art form, needs to move forwards to survive and grow.

THE BEST OF LUCK!

Glossary

ACE Arts Council England.

Aesthetic Showing sensitivity to the beauty of something.

Acoustic The features or characteristics of a space that determine the audibility or quality of sounds within it.

Amphitheatre An oval or round building with tiers of seats around a central open area.

Appia, Adolph Adolph Appia was a Swiss pioneer of modern stage design. Through the use and control of light intensity, colour and manipulation, Appia created a new perspective of scene design and stage lighting.

Aristophanes A Greek comic dramatist. He is also known as the 'Father of Comedy' and the 'Prince of Ancient Comedy'.

Blocking Movement within a scene that an actor is directed to make. This is sometimes recorded in the script.

Brook, Peter Famous director whose work is inspired by the theories of experimental theatre.

Calls When an actor is called to make their entrance on stage (usually by a member of the stage management team).

Choreography The art of composing a dance and planning or arranging the movements, steps and patterns of dancers.

Chorus A group of actors that act as major participants in or commentators on the main action of the drama. In many ancient Greek plays, the chorus expressed to the audience what the main characters could not say, such as their fears or secrets. The chorus usually communicates in song form but sometimes speak their lines in unison.

Commedia dell'arte A form of improvizational theatre that began in Italy in the sixteenth century. Performances were unscripted, held outside and used few props. Outside Italy the form was also known as 'Italian Comedy'.

Community plays A piece of performance that is written or devised specifically for and performed by a local community.

Craig, Gordon An English modernist theatre practitioner who revolutionized scenic, design and lighting techniques.

Cueing A word or action that is the prompt for a change in lighting, sound or any element related to the drama, e.g. scene, prop or costume change.

Devising To invent or create a performance from ideas or themes.

Dip dyeing Where a garment is dipped into a 'dye bath'. It can either be partially submerged, e.g. just the hem of a dress, or the entire garment can be quickly and repeatedly plunged into the dye.

Dramaturgy In-depth analysis of the social and historical background to a text that will have an impact on the way a production is developed. A dramaturge can also be an objective eye when considering how the production will communicate with the audience.

Dry brushing Used in 'breaking down' or aging costumes. A technique which uses a large dry brush (with a small amount of paint) that makes a subtle difference to the age or appearance of a costume.

Euripides A writer of Greek tragedy. He is considered to have been a significant influence on the creation of 'New Comedy' in ancient Greece.

185

Fabula atellana Both a Roman drama and the earliest form of native farce in ancient Italy.

Flying bars Used to 'fly' (i.e. move) items of scenery in and out during a performance.

Folklore The traditional beliefs, legends or customs of a people or groups of people.

Front of house Refers to the portion of the building or space that is open to the public. In the theatre, it typically refers to the auditorium and foyer, as opposed to the stage and backstage areas.

Get-in/get-out When an entire production is either brought in and assembled or dismantled and taken out of a venue or space.

Gobo A metal cut-out disc located in the front of a lamp to project an image on to the stage.

Green Man The Green Man is interpreted as an ancient symbol of re-birth or 'renaissance' and represents the cycle of growth each spring.

Ground plan An aerial view of a venue or space. It may include the design for the set, props or entrance and exits.

Hall, Sir Peter Famous theatre director who is best known for his work with the Royal Shakespeare Company, which he founded in 1960. He served as its artistic director until 1968 and was director of the Royal National Theatre from 1973 to 1988.

Holding area Where the cast are held when not on stage.

Iconic styles A representational interpretation of a style or element rather than a literal one.

Improvization To create something spoken, written or composed without prior preparation.

In-house Denotes that the work is being carried out by the theatre or company staff and not by an outside contractor.

Installation Uses sculptural materials (or other media) to modify the way a particular space is experienced.

Intermission or interval The time between the action of a play or parts of a public performance. It is usually a period of approximately ten to fifteen minutes.

Invisible theatre A form of performance in which the show takes place where people would not normally expect to see one, e.g. in the street or a shopping centre. It is generally recognized to have originally been developed by Augusto Boal, as part of his 'Theater of the Oppressed'.

Jonson, Ben An English Renaissance dramatist, poet and actor. A contemporary of William Shakespeare, he is best known for his satirical plays.

Kabuki theatre A form of traditional Japanese theatre, Kabuki is known for the stylization of its drama and for the elaborate make-up worn by some of its performers.

Kimble tag gun A device commonly used to attach price tags to clothing.

Marlowe, Christopher An English dramatist and poet of the Elizabethan era. The foremost Elizabethan tragedian before William Shakespeare, he is renowned for his blank verse and overreaching protagonists.

Mock-ups An element of the production that is made in rough form for use during the rehearsal period or as a guide to see how it might work during the actual performance, e.g. a prop, costume or piece of set.

Model box A final design scaled-down model that fully demonstrates a design proposal in accurate scale, colour and use.

Non-venues A space or area that is not traditionally used for performance.

Paganism Paganism is a spiritual way of life, which has its roots in the ancient nature religions of the world.

Pageant An elaborate public spectacle that illustrates the history of a place, institution or special occasion. It is often represented in dramatic form or as a procession of floats or costumes.

Papier-mâché A technique to make an object from paper, which is mixed with glue (or other materials) and then pressed together.

Plastazote   A type of polyethylene foam that is mouldable, durable and waterproof. It can be used to create large, lightweight structures and is available in a range of colours and thicknesses.

Practitioner   Someone who practises a profession or particular technique.

Promenade performance   Takes place when the audience are 'guided' around the space to view the action in different locations, often standing rather than seated.

Props   All on-stage furniture, artefacts and set dressing that is not part of the structure of the set.

Proscenium arch   An open-framed wall that divides the acting area from the auditorium. It is usually a large archway at or near the front of the stage, through which the audience views the action. The main stage is the space behind the proscenium arch, often marked by a curtain.

Rake   This is the slope of a stage (or performing area), where the front of the stage is lower than the back. An anti-rake reverses the slope so the back of the stage is lower than the front.

Re-enactments   The recreation of an ancient or historical episode, being as true to the original event as possible.

Revolve   A circular section of the stage flooring, which turns to reveal new scenes.

Ripstop   A lightweight nylon fabric with interwoven re-enforcement threads in a cross-hatch pattern (so the material resists ripping or tearing). It is waterproof and fire-resistant and is the primary material used in hot air balloons.

Role-play   To assume the attitudes, actions and discourse of someone else.

Satire   The use of irony, sarcasm, ridicule (or other methods) to expose or denounce someone or something.

Shaman   A person who acts as an intermediary between the natural and supernatural worlds.

Site-generic   A piece of work or performance that is designed to work in different generic sites. These sites must share a commonality between them, e.g. a beach, a hill or by water.

Site-specific   A piece of work that is designed for a specific location. It can take into account the history, flora or fauna, any myths or legends and geographical location of the site.

Sound effects   Any artificially created or enhanced sound, which is neither narrative nor music.

Soundscapes   Ambient noise that acts as a sound 'backdrop' to a performance or piece of work.

Spectacle   Performances where the draw for an audience is an impressive visual accomplishment.

Stanislavski, Konstantin   A Russian actor and director known as the 'Father of Modern Psychological Acting'. He developed a system of acting known as 'Method' or the 'Stanislavski System'.

Steel deck   A portable staging system, which incorporates a steel framework with a plywood surface for instant staging.

Storyboard   A series of visuals or pictures set out in sequence, showing the plot line of the performance or piece.

Symbolism   The practice of representing things by symbols, or of investing something with a symbolic meaning or character.

Trap doors   An opening in a stage floor, which allows for entrances and exits below the stage.

Wings   The side of a stage where the set ends and the off-stage area begins.

Withy   The name given to strong, flexible willow stems.

LIST OF SUPPLIERS

ART MATERIALS

Acrylics; glaze; metallic paints; spraymount; varnish
Atlantis European Ltd, 7–9 Plumbers Row, London E1 1EQ
(www.atlantisart.co.uk)

Brodie and Middleton, 68 Drury Lane, London WC2B 5SP
(www.brodies.net)

Wet strength tissue paper
Economy of Brighton, 82 St Georges Road, Brighton BN2 1EF
(www.economyofbrighton.co.uk)

Textile medium
Selectasine Serigraphics, 65 Chislehurst Road, Kent BR7 5NP
(www.selectasine.com)

Spray paints
A. Algeo, Sheriden House, Speke Hall Rd, Liverpool L24 9HB
(www.algeos.com)

POLYSTYRENE

Also special contact adhesive
Advanced Fabrication (Manchester Office), Unit 58, Pioneer Mill, Milltown St, Radcliffe, Manchester M26 1WN
Advanced Fabrication (Southend Office), 25 Towerfield Rd, Shoeburyness, Southend-on-Sea SS3 9QT
(www.advanced-pp.co.uk)

PLASTAZOTE

Kewell Converters, 60 Holmethorpe Ave, Redhill, Surrey RH1 2NL
(www.kewell-converters.co.uk)

Zotefoams, 675 Mitcham Road, Croydon, CR9 3AL
(www.zotefoams.com)

Pentonville Rubber, 104–106 Pentonville Road, N1 9JB, London
(pentonvillerubber.co.uk)

WITHY OR WILLOW

Willow Withies, Willow Farm, Ashby Road, Derbyshire, DE12 6DP
(www.willowwithies.co.uk)

Jacobs, Young, Westbury Ltd
(www.jyw-uk.com)

Slimbridge Wetland Plants (JPR Environmental), Breadstone Business Centre, Breadstone, Berkeley, Gloucestershire GL13 9HF
(www.jprwillow.co.uk)

MAKEUP SUPPLIES

Charles Fox, 22 Tavistock Street, London WC2E 7PY
Tel: 0870 2000369
(www.charlesfox.co.uk)

FABRICS

Rip stop
Fabrics-n-stuff, 45 St Austell Road, Weston-super-Mare, BS22 8LJ
(www.fabrics-n-stuff.co.uk)

Canvas
Gerriets (www.gerriets.com)

Powernet and canvas
Whaleys (Bradford) Ltd, Harris Court, Great Horton, Bradford, West Yorkshire, BD7 4EQ
(www.whaleys-bradford.ltd.uk)

Spandex
Borovick Fabrics, 16 Berwick Street, London W1F 0HP
Tel: 02074372180

Spandex House, 263w 38th Street, New York, NY 10018 USA

Wadding
Curtains for You, 24 Queens Road, Hastings, East Sussex, TN34 2JW
Tel: 01424 460840

Tulle
Nevtex, P.O.Box 87, Nottingham NG1 1LP

HABERDASHERY

Kleins, 5 Noel St, London, WIF 8GD
Tel: 02074376162
(www.kleins.co.uk)

McCulloch and Wallis, 25–26 Dering Steet, London, W1S 1AT
(www.macculloch-wallis.co.uk)

THEATRE SUPPLIES

Copydex; Evostick; FEV; Flambar; fuller's earth; heat guns; Idendon/Satgecoat; powder colour; PVA glue; Rosco paint; Rub'n'buff; vapour masks; soldering irons

Brian Joseph Hardware, 2 Hereward Road, London SW17 7EY
(www.bjhardware.com)

Flint Hire and Supply, Queens Row, London, SE17 2PX
(www.flints.co.uk)

SCULPTING SUPPLIES

Aluminium mesh
Tiranti, 70 High St, Theale, Reading, Berks RG7 5AR
(www.tiranti.co.uk)

Kimble tag guns
56 Great Titchfield Street, London, W1W 7DF
(www.morplan.com)

Steel deck
30 Arklow Road, Deptford, London, SE14 6EB
(www.steeldeck.co.uk)

Wango's Staging Concepts, Old Station House, Ingham, Bury St Edmonds, Suffolk, IP31 1NS
(www.wangos.com)

Barriers
Events Solutions Ltd (www.stagebarriers.co.uk)
Old CoatesRoad, Throapham, Sheffield, Yorkshire, S25 2QX

Truck track
Ten 47 Limited, Unit 2B, Frances Industrial Park, Wemyss Road, Dysart, Kirkcaldy, Fife
(www.ten47.com)

Tempower, 10 Helions Park Gardens, Haverhill, Suffolk, CB9 8BW
(www.tempower.co.uk)

Wheels
Machine Mart
(www.machinemart.co.uk)

INDEX